Parenting
THE
OFFICE

Parenting
THE
OFFICE

By Doris S. Davidoff, Philip G. Davidoff,
Donald M. Davidoff, and Douglas G. Davidoff

Foreword by J. W. Marriott, Jr.

PELICAN PUBLISHING COMPANY
Gretna 2001

*The word "Pelican" and the depiction of a pelican are trademarks
of Pelican Publishing Company, Inc., and are registered in the
U.S. Patent and Trademark Office.*

Library of Congress Cataloging-in-Publication Data

Parenting the office / Doris S. Davidoff ... [et al.].
   p. cm.
  ISBN 1-56554-820-5 (alk. paper)
   1. Personnel management. 2. Management. 3. Parenting. 4. Psychology, Industrial. 5.
Child psychology. I. Davidoff, Doris S.

  HF5549 .P249 2001
  158.7—dc21

                                                  00-069871

Cartoons by John Klossner

Printed in the United States of America
Published by Pelican Publishing Company, Inc.
1000 Burmaster Street, Gretna, Louisiana 70053

We dedicate Parenting the Office *to the next generation*
of Davidoffs, Erika, Drew, Daria, and Dylan.
May the spirit of learning and the love of good work
be as strong in you as it has been in your parents and grandparents.

Contents

Part II: Proven Parenting Techniques Every Manager Should Master

Foreword

Parenting the Office is a powerful juxtaposition of what appears at first glance to be two completely separate worlds. In reality, parenting and the workplace are closely related.

As chairman of Marriott International, I've always operated on the belief that if we take good care of our associates, they will take good care of our customers and customers will come back. How do we take care of our associates? We nurture them, help them grow, and make them feel important. We teach them positive behaviors and instill in them the self-esteem and confidence to make the right choices—even when those are the toughest.

It sounds an awful lot like what we do as parents, doesn't it?

Since I was born in the 1930s, I've had the pleasure and privilege of watching (and ultimately presiding over) the growth of our family's business. From a small root-beer stand my parents founded a few years before I was born, we've grown to what is now one of the most successful companies in the hospitality industry. Just as importantly, I've had the pleasure (and faced the challenge) of raising four children.

I'm often not sure which was more difficult, but I'm constantly reminded of the similarities between the two. The things it took to teach my children the values that matter in life—honesty, the importance of hard work, loyalty—are the same things it takes to teach these values to associates at Marriott. People are the essence of any social unit, whether we're talking about parents and children at home or managers and associates at work, so this shouldn't be at all surprising.

The Davidoffs, in the book you are about to read, have done a wonderful job of weaving the similarities between home and office together. As you read through the book, you're likely to picture you and your associates in exactly the situations the Davidoffs present. *Parenting the Office* is a modern guide to understanding and implementing proven parenting principles in your office to increase your personal and your organization's success.

I trust that you will find it as useful as I have.

J. W. MARRIOTT, JR.

Preface

Being a woman without an advanced business degree wasn't a challenge. Raising children by myself taught me what I needed to know to manage a business. If you can get people to remember the golden rule, to work and play together, and to share their toys, you can be successful.

—Judith Resnick
CEO of The Resnick Group and a former
CEO of an investment banking and brokerage firm

In the 1960s, we started our family. Shortly after that, we started our first business, a travel agency in Bowie, Maryland. Since then, we've run several businesses in the travel industry, including a travel school and a travel-agency franchise group. Over that time, we have employed a wide variety of people, some of whom worked with us for more than twenty years. Our three children, two of whom are co-authors of this book, ranged from one to four and a half years of age at the time we started the business. Since the 1970s, we've taught numerous management seminars to owners and managers of small businesses and to managers of offices within larger companies.

As we raised our children at the same time as managing our employees, we were constantly struck by the similarities between many of their behaviors. At seminars, we found ourselves answering questions by relating what should be done in families while raising children.

Some questions in seminars and in our own day-to-day business operations seemed more like parenting questions than "business" questions. For example, what should we do about two equivalent employees, one of whom was always willing to help out with whatever had to be done, and the other who always seemed to be "busy" with something else whenever help was needed with a task not specifically assigned? This reminded us of exactly the situation a good friend of ours had. She had two daughters—one who always offered to help clear the table and do the dishes after dinner, the other who somehow always suddenly remembered that she had to do her homework or study for a test tomorrow. Our friend took the easy way. She never confronted her shirker and just assumed the "willing" daughter didn't really care.

Unfortunately, the willing daughter did care. She just didn't verbalize it. As the resentment built up, she began to hate her sister and believe her mother liked her sister more. It took a major trauma—she ran away from home at the age of sixteen—to bring this issue to the forefront and force our friend to deal with it. We found relating this parenting analogy to the behavior of these two employees was a much more effective way to offer management advice than any discussion about "conflict management," "MBO" (Management by Objectives), or whatever other idea *du jour* was popular. In a way, *Parenting the Office* was born.

By the time we actually decided to sit down and put it all on paper, our sons were grown and had become quite experienced in business management and consulting themselves. Donald now manages teams of developers at Manugistics, an industry-leading software company in the cutting-edge disciplines of pricing and revenue optimization and supply-chain management, and Douglas is a financial consultant with industry-leading Merrill Lynch. Donald started in the air force as a project manager, and Douglas began his career with two of the leading rental-car companies in North America. Like so many in the business world, Donald and Doug are office "parents" in their management and guidance of others, while they are also office "children," as they are subordinate to higher-level managers.

The concepts involved in *Parenting the Office* really crystallized during the six-year period that the four of us started, built, and sold a travel-agency franchise group. We were able to put many of our ideas to work in building our own team and helping other businesses build theirs. Working together combined the perceptions and beliefs of both the "parent" and the "child" generations, and the result is what you see in this book.

Now that our children are raising families of their own, the whole experience is coming full circle! We welcome your interest in this subject, and we invite you to share your ideas, thoughts, and stories. Visit us at www.parentingtheoffice.com or email us at feedback@parentingtheoffice.com. We look forward to hearing from you!

Acknowledgments

Obviously, a book of this nature doesn't come together without the help of many people. First, we'd like to thank Dana Davidoff, the third sibling of the Davidoff family. Though she isn't a co-author of this book, her experiences, ideas, and support helped give this book that much more life.

Writing this book took many hours. Since Donald and Doug have full-time jobs and families with young children, it took a lot of time away from their families. So we are most appreciative of the sacrifices their respective wives, Yvonne Davidoff and Dani Davidoff, made to support this effort. Not only did they contribute ideas of their own, but perhaps more importantly they constantly ran interference to keep the little third-generation Davidoffs at bay while "Daddy had to work on the computer."

Once a book is written, unfortunately the hard work begins—editing! A big thanks goes to Marilyn Kessler, a longtime family friend and business partner, and to Virginia Seaborn, a colleague of Donald's, who took their own time to review many of the chapters and to provide story ideas of their own.

Perhaps most importantly, we'd like to thank everyone we've worked with.

Each person, in their own way, knowingly or not, contributed to our understanding of how offices work like families. At the businesses we've owned and operated, Belair Travel & Cruises, Capital Area Travel Academy, and VALU Travel Marketing; the government organizations we've worked in, the Federal Aviation Administration and the United States Air Force Ballistic Missile Division; the other companies we've worked in, American Society of Travel Agents (ASTA), Talus Solutions, Manugistics, Alamo, Hertz, and Merrill Lynch; and the many companies with whom we've consulted, we've always learned something that contributed to the ideas in this book. Without these experiences, we never could have written this book!

We would also like to thank the people at Pelican Publishing, especially Nina Kooij, without whose faith and enthusiasm this book could never have become a reality and whose guidance and editing made this a better book.

Lastly, but very importantly, we want to thank our cartoonist, John Klossner. We have enjoyed working with him and highly appreciate the spirit he added to *Parenting the Office.*

Introduction

Have you ever felt as though your employees were your kids; that as a boss, manager, or supervisor you behaved like a parent; or that your staff sometimes acted like children or siblings?

That's why you should read this book! It's about home as a metaphor for workplace and family as a metaphor for management and employees. In reality, many of us spend more waking hours with our staff than we do with our actual (or home) family. We may even think of our employees as our second family. It is, therefore, important to understand the relationships among both the home and office "family" members. These relationships are amazingly similar.

We have all recognized what may appear to be "childish" behavior in the office—yet, upon closer examination, we can just as easily describe these behaviors with the same terms we would use to describe sibling rivalry, peer pressure, middle-child syndrome, etc. These behaviors, it turns out, are not necessarily childish. Rather, they are manifestations of normal social relationships that are as old as families themselves. They are the same reactions that have been imprinted on us from our earliest memories. In short, they're human—just as we are.

There are, of course, a number of differences between children in a family and employees in an office. Employees can quit; children generally don't have that option. Managers can fire employees; parents generally don't have that option. The office tends to have a wider range of backgrounds, personalities, and ages than a family. But if you've ever experienced the déjà vu of finding a situation in the office remarkably similar to a previous family experience, then you already know that these are differences of form more than substance.

In this book, we share with you many of the anecdotes that have helped us effectively manage our businesses and that have become the bedrock of the consulting advice we give many of our clients. This is not a book just about relationships. It is a book about how we can make these relationships work to increase the functionality of our office environment so employees and managers look forward to working with their fellow employees. Ultimately, the office becomes more effective.

"Part I: Family Dynamics at Play in the Office" focuses on the "children." Through chapters on the challenges of sibling rivalry, siblings and a common enemy, the "oldest" child, etc., we discuss how a variety of well-understood family situations relate to real-world office situations. We examine these similarities with an eye towards helping managers see these behaviors in a new light. Understanding the situations and then recognizing when they're happening to you is the first step towards being able to make the office a more effective "working family." When you're done reading this part, you are better equipped to realize what is really happening in your office and which approaches are most likely to work for you.

"Part II: Proven Parenting Techniques Every Manager Should Master" focuses more on the "parents" and how to apply specific parenting techniques that we have found work just as well in the office. This includes the need to understand the differences among the children, avoiding trying to be a "super" or "perfect" parent, and the challenges of the "single" parent, who is the sole manager in the office. This last one is particularly important to the growing ranks of small-business owners; though with the ever-constant drive towards efficiency in large corporations, even traditional middle managers feel more alone and out on a proverbial island than ever.

At the end of each chapter, there are tips for managers given from the perspective of other managers as well as tips for managers from the perspective of their employees.

Whether you're a manager, someone who plans to become a manager, or a frontline employee with no intentions of becoming a manager, this book will help you work more effectively with your office "family" and make your working experience more fulfilling and enjoyable.

We do not pretend to claim that we are presenting revolutionary new ideas that no one has ever thought of in the past. Spencer Johnson, co-author of *The One Minute Manager,* later wrote *One Minute Parenting,* a discussion we think of as "managing the home." Seminal self-help guru Stephen R. Covey has written books on the office, the home, and the self. However, though many have related stories about family to stories at the office and vice versa, few if any have directly applied proven parenting techniques to the office environment the way this book does.

By taking a new and different look at these ideas, and by using suggestions and behaviors with which we are all familiar but maybe never thought pertained to groups of adults working closely together, these "old" ideas can take on a new meaning and give you the ability to act more effectively. What we've heard from the people who have attended our seminars on this topic, and hope to hear from you as well, is "This makes so much sense, I can't believe it hasn't been said before." You will agree with many of the things we say and point out in this book, and you may even disagree with some. Should you experience the latter, we suggest you take the advice that Doug heard once at a seminar and that all four of us agree is a great way to approach any set of new ideas or new learning experiences. "Take the best, and leave the rest."

To bring more life to the ideas, we've sprinkled the book not only with our own observations but also with many stories from our experience. Each story is set apart from the rest of the text by italics. Each begins with the name of which of us is actually telling the story. All references to ourselves are 100 percent accurate, and the stories themselves are also true. However, we have changed the names of anyone else involved so as to protect their privacy.

We've written *Parenting the Office* in a straightforward, easy-to-read, enjoyable manner that should help you to become a more effective manager. You will see many of your prior co-workers or managers in this book. You may even see yourself!

Parenting
THE
OFFICE

PART I

Family Dynamics at Play in the Office

CHAPTER 1

Sibling Rivalry: Employee Jealousy

If sisters were free to express how they really feel, parents would hear this: "Give me all the attention and all the toys and send Rebecca to live with Grandma." —Linda Sunshine
Mom Loves Me Best
(And Other Lies You Told Your Sister)

Doris and Phil

At one seminar, a member of the audience, Susan, related to us how, when she was raising two kids, she bought them each a truck. They were exactly the same, except that one was red and one was blue. Without thinking much about it, she gave the blue one to her older son, John, and the red one to her younger child, Jim. Jim immediately wanted the blue truck—as best she could figure only because John had it. Meanwhile, John noticed a small nick on Jim's red truck and, thus, would have nothing to do with it. Susan thought, "Sometimes you get punished for trying to do something nice." She finished her story by saying the irony was that only recently she had returned from a trip to Europe with a variety of small gifts to share with her "office family"—her employees. The resulting hassle over who got what made her wish she'd never bought anything to bring back.

Childish? She thought so, but we pointed out it was simply human!

You've seen it a thousand times. One person in the office gets something, and another feels slighted. You may even have felt it yourself. "Why didn't I get that?" you think, or "I'm just as good as they are." Usually it doesn't really bother us; but no matter how mature we are, it's still there.

23

Donald

One company we worked with had grown through mergers and increased sales to the point where the Human Resources Department came up with an idea to increase morale and employee retention. At the next annual meeting, they would award a watch to everyone who was celebrating their five-year anniversary with the company. Great idea—so what's the problem?

Our primary contact on this consulting project was a very capable mid-level analyst who had worked her way up in the company. She was celebrating her six-year anniversary that year and therefore didn't qualify. She confessed to us that, though she didn't even need a watch, she was a bit miffed that she was, in effect, "penalized" for being a loyal six-year employee rather than someone celebrating their fifth year.

Was this going to cause her to hate her job or, worse, quit? Of course not. But through a simple oversight and insensitivity as to how decisions about one group of employees affect another, this company turned an effort designed to increase morale into something that resulted in mixed feelings on the part of employees. Instead of feeling closer, this employee felt more distant from "the company."

More has been written about sibling rivalry than virtually any other family dynamic. Like death and taxes, it is inevitable. If you have more than one child, you have sibling rivalry. Even if you're an only child, you understand sibling rivalry exists between brothers and sisters. Regardless of how illogical it may be, it is always affecting people's behavior (whether they're thirteen, thirty-five, or seventy).

Donald and Doug

As we grew up and went to college, we both noticed an interesting phenomenon. As kids, we had more than our fair share of sibling rivalry. But as first Donald, then Doug, went off to college, we just assumed that was a phase we'd leave behind in our childhood.

When we were apart from each other, we had no problems, and our relationship was much more mature. But whenever the family got back together, all the old feelings would come back. It didn't seem to matter what the issue was. Back in the familiar surroundings of home, we went right at it again. The ingrained pattern repeated.

Over the years, we learned that our behavior wasn't so much childish as childlike. And we saw this same basic pattern repeat in our workplaces. As we've risen to various levels of middle or upper management of businesses small and large, we see that peers at work exhibit the same sibling rivalry we felt—even years after they've moved on or up. And we've realized it really shouldn't be expected to be any other way.

Sibling rivalry is not a dynamic that happens only in the home. In the office, it often gets misdiagnosed as simply immaturity on the part of employees. Sibling rivalry in and of itself is neither good nor bad—many times rivalry can be a positive motivating force. The issue is how it is manifested and to what degree it exists. Many successful sales organizations learned the beneficial powers of sibling rivalry in the contests and rewards programs that they have implemented. When Donald had a co-worker review one of the early drafts of this chapter, she commented how fondly she remembered looking up to her brother and working hard to be able to "beat him" in anything she could. She felt that it made her a stronger, better person.

An Office Must Work as a Team

As a manager, you need to learn to deal with sibling rivalry to develop an effective team. As a matter of fact, if you think that your office is not exhibiting sibling rivalry, then you've got a problem. Either you're not being perceptive about what is happening in your office, or the people there don't feel attached enough to the office to care about where they stand in the pecking order.

However, when the level of competition between siblings becomes severe, it can destroy the entire team. There is no room for jealousy or unhealthy competitive forces within a group of people who must work together and produce meaningful results.

That's why it is critical that all members of our "family," whether at home or in the office, work together to watch for the first signs of unhealthy rivalry that can hurt the group. Then we must work together to eliminate the rivalry or make it a healthy one. A healthy rivalry fosters a friendly and positive competitive spirit, bringing out the creative best in all of us.

Doris and Phil

As mentioned earlier, when Doug and Donald were growing up, they exhibited intense sibling rivalry—not surprising for two boys separated by twenty-eight months. Even (perhaps especially) in unimportant things like ping pong or pool, Doug would try his best to beat his older brother, and

"We normally view competition in the office as a positive motivational force, Johnson, but in this case I think we have a problem."

Donald would be darned if he'd let him. Continued prodding from his parents wouldn't get Donald to cut his brother any slack. As they got older and went off to school and their first jobs, the intensity subsided; but as soon as they were together again at holidays or any other family get-together, all the old rivalry bubbled right back to the surface.

When we were putting our VALU Travel Marketing business together, we were very concerned about whether this would be an issue. Could Doug and Donald work together day in and day out in a cooperative and positive way? Sure, they said they could, but it's much more easily said than done. Sibling rivalry often operates at a level below the purely conscious one, and it can be difficult to separate from real issues. After all, one person's "suggesting a better way to do something" could be another person's "continued petty one-upmanship."

What happened was a lesson in how sibling rivalry can be a positive force in an office. The boys were still competitive. Each had his own ideas and wanted his opinion to win the day, much as anyone wants to be important to the success of any team endeavor. However, they came to respect each other's strengths and, perhaps more importantly, no longer viewed each other's weaknesses as targets for exploitation.

Donald has always been very analytically oriented and an excellent developer of business processes but has usually shied away from direct sales. He understands the sales process, but prefers to contribute to strategy rather than execution. Doug has always been an excellent salesman but tends not to want to get bogged down in the details of operation. He understands the importance of getting the details done; he'd just prefer someone else do it. They both are good at marketing and enjoy it, which really could have been a problem.

Donald became our VP, Member Services while Doug became VP, Business Development. They developed an approach where they shared their ideas with each other but deferred to each other's responsibility and authority for their respective departments. Instead of constantly fighting over marketing direction (the one area they both were expert at), they respected the fact that each approached the issue from a different perspective. They realized that this represented an opportunity to share. They ultimately developed the procedure that we would not make a major decision unless both agreed, since either one having a problem with an idea meant something was probably wrong with it.

Make no mistake about it, it was not simple or easy to get to this point. Their idea of "sharing" views could be pretty loud and, at times, confrontational. Just ask any of our employees from that time. But all of the arguing was merely noise, though it may not have always felt that way at the time. Underneath, there was a deep and growing mutual respect and a realization that they were better as a team than the sum of the two individual parts. That's sibling rivalry as synergy—competition built on a foundation of cooperation, with this "co-opetition" fueling the growth of both them and the business.

Donald

Contrast this with a brother and sister, Tom and Judy, we worked with who had taken over a two-office travel agency from their parents when their parents retired. Judy was older, an excellent operations person, and one of the finest travel agents we ever had the pleasure to meet. But she was often abrupt, demanding, and really didn't enjoy marketing and managing a small business in the modern age of large agencies, the Internet, etc.

Tom was very interested in the marketing and management side. He often looked as if he was paying less attention to detail than he was, and whenever he dropped the ball on something, it made it seem even worse. He understood the need to change the agency's approach and was the motivating force behind seeking us out.

There was obviously sibling rivalry in place as Judy and Tom each positioned decisions to win the acceptance of their parents, who were still

40 percent owners and had to approve any major decisions. Judy never got past looking at Tom as "the baby of the family who could never get it right" and couldn't possibly have ideas better than hers. Tom, on the other hand, could never get past his resentment of Judy's firstborn advantages.

Both siblings discussed their strengths and weaknesses and acknowledged the dynamics at play. Even with this knowledge, they couldn't get past their existing dysfunctional relationship. The agency was suffering and they were both miserable, but any perceived slight from the other was viewed as cause to no longer even try. It was the classic blame game, "it's her/his fault, not mine," while the real goal—profitability—slipped away. At one point, they didn't even talk to each other for two months, instead sending messages through employees, their parents, and us. It was very difficult for us to maintain a neutral, facilitator position as each sought validation from us that they were "more right."

It got to the point where our recommendation became "get a business divorce." Simply put, they would have either needed to break up the business or break up the family.

While these two stories involve actual siblings and occurred at the managerial level (in both instances the managers were in the role of co-workers), the stories apply equally well to co-workers who are not related and/or not in a management role. When thinking about sibling rivalry in an office, remember that all members of your office family have a history of their own in their relationships with siblings. Some may have been only children with no such experience. The office will be their only direct experience of the give-and-take that sibling relationships require. Some have been the oldest child, while others grew up as the baby in the family. We've certainly seen how the three children in our family approach things differently, often based on their experiences with sibling rivalry as they grew up.

The office family has another complication since there is often a variety of chronological ages. Many times, an older employee reports to a younger one. More often, company "equals" will have a wide disparity in their age.

Sibling rivalry can strike in what appears to managers to be very strange ways. One company we worked with had what, on the surface, seemed to be almost a laughable experience—but the result was no joke to the manager involved.

Doris
In this case, the manager, Jessica, had a problem employee, Martha.

Martha often took two hours to accomplish one hour's work, made frequent mistakes, spent too much time on personal calls, etc. Jessica thought she had a great solution. She moved Martha to the desk next to hers. This allowed her to keep a close eye on Martha and make immediate corrections to any inappropriate behavior. It would also serve as a deterrent for things like making personal phone calls since Martha's actions were so visible to her.

If anything, Jessica viewed this change of Martha's location as a punishment. Some of the other people in the office, however, actually viewed it as a perk to have so much "face time" with the manager. Within a couple of months, her best employee, Elizabeth, left. During an exit interview, Jessica found that the desk-location situation had played heavily in Elizabeth's feeling that Jessica cared more about Martha than about anyone else.

Was this an immature response? Perhaps, but it was also perfectly human—especially when interpreted in the context of sibling rivalry. More importantly, Jessica had lost one of her best people because she didn't look at the situation through the eyes of the "office siblings."

In another consulting engagement, we saw another cause of sibling rivalry: a new "child."

Doug

I was working with the sales manager of a company who had just expanded his outside sales force. He was the real "rah-rah" type. He'd been a great salesperson himself, and this was his first foray into management, so he was very excited. He would talk up the new person and really focus his attention on what was happening, trying to get him up to speed as quickly as possible.

The problem was that he "forgot" his other salesperson. The other salesperson had been with the manager since the manager had started. He did a good job and, frankly, didn't need a lot of attention. The perceived slight, however, drove him crazy. He didn't know what to do, and, when a new opportunity came along, he left the company.

The manager didn't mean to slight the senior salesperson; he just forgot how he had felt when he was a child and his new brother got all the attention.

Was the "neglect" the only reason for leaving? Of course not, but he was clearly threatened by the presence of a new "office sibling" in what had been a "one child" office family. When parents have new children, the existing children can resent the loss of attention, but they can't quit the family. "Office siblings," however, can quit. When threatened, a normal reaction is "fight or flight," and this employee chose the flight option.

Dealing with Sibling Rivalry

So, how do you deal effectively with sibling rivalry? Communicate. It works in the office just as well as it works in a family. In our story about the start of VALU Travel Marketing, the key to Doug's and Don's getting along was that they spent the time up front to communicate their goals and concerns. As a result, they made sure that they always had the same end result in mind (albeit, with a few loud discussions in the interim).

Had the manager who moved the employee's desk more effectively communicated her appreciation of the other employees who were working well, they would not have misinterpreted the move as a slight against them. Had the sales manager been more aware of how his senior salesperson felt threatened, or better communicated why he was taking so much time with the new employee, he may not have lost that senior salesperson.

Doris and Phil

While raising our children, we found that family meetings were often a way to address specific behaviors in an indirect "this is what is expected of everyone" approach rather than directly confronting the offending member of the family. These meetings had the added benefit of promoting some sibling pressure to keep everyone in line. We found that the same technique frequently worked in the office.

Staff meetings, like family meetings, can often be used to encourage behavioral changes. Managers, the "office parents," can share their views in a nonconfrontational way. Employees, the "office siblings," can feel part of the decision-making process and share ways to improve communication and performance. More importantly, you can use these meetings to "share the vision"—to make sure that all employees understand the company goals and how they are helping to make these goals a reality. Too often, staff meetings are used as an opportunity to tell everyone what is going wrong. They are much more effective when you tell everyone what's going right. The result is that sibling pressure may end up keeping everyone in line better than any managers could ever do on their own.

Some of the most common examples of sibling rivalry are related to perks or opportunities within the office. We discussed earlier the situation in one office where a desk position near the manager was misinterpreted. An even more common situation in corporate America is the size and position of an office. Co-workers can fight over a window office just as kids fight over who gets the window seat in the car or on an airplane. If you are a manager, you must be very careful to distribute perceived perks fairly.

Whether or not something is actually a "perk" doesn't matter. If employees think it is special, it is. It's your responsibility to be aware of what your employees consider perks. You might not even have thought of the fact that they consider the desk by the window to have a higher status than the other desks. Or you might assume that moving an employee to what you consider to be a more prestigious location is a reward. However, asking an employee to move can create stress. People get attached to a location, just as children are attached to "their" place at the table or "their" room. They may resent a sibling who caused the change. Even today, our three adult children, who have lived on their own for years, will still try to sit at "their" seats at our dinner table when they eat in our home. They also still refer to "their" rooms, even though these rooms were converted to a guestroom or storage room for years.

Remember, "good" and "bad" perks are from the employees' perspective.

Doris and Phil

When our children were young, as in most families with three children, there was usually a fight over who was stuck in the middle seat in the back of the car since everyone wanted a window seat. However, when Donald was eleven or twelve years old, he suddenly realized that the middle seat

"After I won the award, my co-workers thought I should get an office with a better view."

gave him an unobstructed view out the front window. From then on, he went for the middle seat without any argument. This solved the problem for several months. Of course, human nature being what it is, and children being what they are, Doug and Dana began to wonder why he was suddenly so agreeable. "There must be something to this middle seat," they thought. Although they didn't know why he now wanted the middle seat, they began to want it too. The arguments started again, only now they were over who got the middle seat and who was "stuck" with the window seat. To this day, we remind Donald how he caused us to go from having two out of three kids happy to two out of three upset!

People remember every time someone else got something they wanted and forget most times when they were given something others wanted. Children exclaim, "You always let her do it," or "You never let me do it!" Although employees will rarely be so obvious, they have similar memories. This is not being childish—it is merely a natural human reaction. Again, it is not the frontline workers' responsibility to maintain fairness in the office. It is management's.

However, fair does not mean that everyone gets an equal portion of everything. When our children were young, we tried to make sure that anytime we gave one a gift or saw something special for them (unless it was for a birthday), we got something for the others. We tried to make sure all gifts were either the same number of packages or, as they got older and more aware of the price rather than the quantity, that the values were equal.

However, our experience was no different from Susan's in our opening story. Ultimately, we realized that even this did not reduce rivalry. We were better off trying to be relatively fair rather than totally fair, since there is no such thing as totally fair, especially in the eyes of the recipients. No matter how equal parents try to make things, siblings will each see the situation from their own vantage points and will notice the slightest differences—things you didn't even see.

Mom always liked you best!   —Tommy Smothers (circa 1968)

Tips from Managers

1. Recognize intra-office rivalries for what they are—normal human behavior.

2. Reasonable intra-office competition brings out the best in people.

3. Office behavior with co-workers is often a reenactment of how employees behaved with their siblings. Learning about an employee's relationship with their own family can help you understand how they relate to others in the office.

4. Use staff meetings like family meetings. They are a chance to air important issues and constructive criticisms without specifically confronting individuals and making them defensive. Use these meetings to get employee feedback on what is bothering or pleasing them.

5. Look at "perks" through your employees' eyes, not yours.

6. Equality and fairness are in the eyes of the observer, so it is impossible for everyone to believe you are fair all of the time. Do your best and keep communication open.

7. Facilitate the resolution of disputes, don't referee them.

8. Don't try to overmanage. More problems result from managers trying to do too much than from managers not doing enough.

9. Put policies in writing to increase your ability to make consistent decisions.

10. *Communicate!* This includes listening.

Tips from Employees

1. Don't make decisions based on which one of us is asking, but rather on what your answer would be to any of us.

2. Be consistent. We get confused when we don't know what to expect.

3. Have written policies and give all of us a copy or keep a copy in a place convenient to all of us. But you better stick to your policies— anything else is hypocritical and moves us towards one-upmanship with our peers.

4. Be willing to tell us why we must or can't do something.

5. Help us understand how each of us fits into the overall plan for the office.

6. Show appreciation to all of us, both as a team and as individuals.

7. If you see one of us doing something wrong, and a general reminder to everyone has been ignored by the guilty one, please discuss the matter privately with the one involved.

8. Don't put us in direct competition with each other. Friendly competition can be fun, but dog-eat-dog competition makes us feel vulnerable. Help us work together.

9. Help us each grow in our responsibilities so we won't get jealous of a sibling who always seems to get the "best" tasks assigned.

10. Don't be so worried about the "negative" aspects of sibling rivalry. We want to compete with our peers and if it's not destructive, let us have our fun.

CHAPTER 2

Siblings and a Common Enemy: Can We Work Together?

All for one, one for all.

—Alexandre Dumas
The Three Musketeers

Doris

One evening, when our children were ages seven to eleven, we had left them in the care of a teenage babysitter whom we had used several times. When we returned home after a movie, they were sound asleep, but our bed was a mess. The spread, blanket, and top sheet were pulled off, and there had obviously been some roughhousing on the bed.

We asked the babysitter what had happened and were informed that Donald, backed up, of course, by his brother and sister, had told her that they were allowed to use our bed as a trampoline. The babysitter actually believed them. We have to admit that, since there was no permanent damage, we were quite impressed that this group of young children could so easily overcome what should have been the common sense of a sixteen-year-old babysitter, and we did get a good laugh out of it. Of course, we did our laughing out of sight of the children or the babysitter. We were, in fact, amazed at the level of cooperation of the typically squabbling siblings, but informed them, somewhat forcefully, not to do it again.

Even the most competitive and argumentative siblings will sometimes come together and work as a team, especially when they have a common enemy. This common enemy could be the parents, a specific other sibling,

35

an outside person, or even an outside event or challenge. The same set of dynamics works within an office environment.

This tendency of competitors to join forces when confronted by a common enemy can be harnessed by those in authority to bring out the best in the group, but it can also cause harm if the group goes down the wrong paths.

The well-known "labor vs. management" dynamic is no different from the "children united against the parents" scenario. What family doesn't find that Bobby and Susie, who are always fighting, suddenly stick up for each other when they might both get in trouble? They agree to tell the same story and back up each other's position. Or they suddenly cooperate and, together, plan some action that conflicts with family policies, hoping that, by acting jointly, they can avoid punishment.

In the story that opened this chapter, the children actually had two common enemies—the parents and the babysitter. In order to gain control, they cooperated. Their collaboration, however, was not particularly beneficial to the family as a whole.

This same spirit of cooperation can be harnessed towards a common purpose that is beneficial to the whole team. Team incentives are more successful because you need everyone's cooperation to achieve a goal. While individual incentives can work when the need is more for specific individual actions than a team effort, they can actually be counterproductive when a team effort is required.

Doris and Phil

Many years ago, we were trying to get our staff to work as a team but also to maximize sales. We set up a system that provided a financial bonus to every employee when the entire office exceeded set quarterly goals. We posted a thermometer on the refrigerator in the lunchroom that tracked each month's progress towards that quarter's goals.

We found that, if the group was lagging behind the goal, the employees who were working hard would encourage or even help the others work more efficiently. They realized that their own bonus was in jeopardy if others in the group didn't produce.

This system worked well for many years. However, in more recent years, after the retirement of our core "old-timer" staff, the needs of the newer, younger staff members changed. We found that two high producers, Dave and Monica, who had worked for us for just a couple of years, were getting very resentful of two other employees, Joe and Ruth, who were producing less and pulling the group down. These two lower-pro-ducing employees had the ability but were satisfied with their salaries and were, more or less, sitting back and not working to their fullest potential. We realized that we were in danger of losing Dave and Monica and keep-ing Joe and Ruth, which would drastically affect our ability to maintain a profit. We couldn't just raise salaries for Dave and Monica without reduc-ing our overall profit, unless we took the additional cost from someone else's salary.

Due to this situation, we drastically changed our compensation pro-gram. We changed to a pay-for-performance basis for our salespeople, so that each salesperson earned an income based directly on actual sales. We made it clear, however, that everyone was expected to pull together to help a client when that client's agent wasn't available. We continued a team-incentive program for the support staff, since they backed up the sales staff without making sales themselves.

The new system resulted in the immediate voluntary resignation of Joe and Ruth and additional, well-earned income for Dave and Monica, which reenergized them and helped them feel appreciated and fairly com-pensated for their efforts. We replaced Joe and Ruth with one new ener-getic employee and kept our overall compensation costs stable.

A Common Enemy Can Be a Positive Force

Sometimes, it even serves managers to become a mild "enemy" to get the team to work together.

Donald

There's nothing like sports to bond teams of subordinates together for a common cause. This is one of the reasons organizations like the military put so much time into athletics. I learned the power of this kind of bond-ing firsthand while running a freshmen orientation program for the air force ROTC during my senior year in college.

The program was very tough—full of marching, drilling, teaching, pop quizzes, etc. The purpose was to make success possible only through teamwork. Part of the environment was designed to create a respect/fear paradigm, almost a love/hate relationship between the cadets and the cadet officers.

On the third day, we scheduled a softball game. The idea was to have a bit of a break from the very formal environment and introduce a little bit of athletics and teamwork at the same time. Just before it was supposed to start, the skies opened up and it began to pour, so we thought quickly and changed it to an indoor game of team dodge ball.

The tournament went extremely well. In the enclosed environment of the gym, the teams played each other vigorously. Those who were knocked out cheered their teammates.

It went so well that we agreed to let the winners play against the staff. Although the four teams had been in fierce direct competition for almost two hours, now they had a common enemy—the officers who were making their lives difficult. This was their one chance, their only way, to exact some revenge. There we were with forty-five freshmen whose teams had lost cheering on the winning team in their challenge against us. That single event did more to bring out teamwork and create morale and a sense of belonging than anything else in the entire five-day program.

Another example of channeling teamwork in a positive direction is the way Phil and Doris handled the children not too long after the bed-as-trampoline incident.

Doris

We made Donald our prime babysitter, at least during short absences. We challenged our children to prove that they could take care of themselves if we went out for a short period. We were the "enemy" to whom they had to prove themselves and Donald was the oldest and the "leader" of the gang. He knew the rules and he knew that we knew he knew the rules. By putting responsibility on his shoulders, we challenged him to prove he could succeed. He didn't want to face us having lost control of the situation, so he turned out to be better at managing his siblings than most of our other babysitters had been.

Phil

A similar situation can occur when a "sibling" in an office is promoted to a management position. In our office several years ago, we had promoted an energetic, capable young woman, Kathie, to assistant manager. Up until then, Kathie had always been "one of the gang." Now she was suddenly one of "them" in the old "us against them" conflict. At first, it was very uncomfortable for her. She suddenly went from being a pal of equal status, who could gripe with her co-workers about what the managers did, to one of the managers, who sometimes had to say no to an employee's request. Kathie had another challenge in that she was still spending a considerable amount of time performing frontline functions side by side with her co-workers.

After a few weeks, Kathie learned to handle this paradox in an interesting but effective manner. She had a little figure of a camel on her desk. The camel had a saddle with a bucket on one side (the bucket from the other side was missing). She told the staff that when the bucket was turned out toward the center of the office, she was wearing her management hat, and when the bucket was turned toward her chair, she was frontline. This not only helped the staff accept her two roles, but let her settle into her management responsibilities more easily. When an employee came to Kathie to ask for permission for vacation time (which was one of her management functions), she would turn the camel with the bucket away from her. The employees realized quickly that this was not the time to use their "pal" relationship to get what they wanted, but to accept whatever response she gave. After a few weeks of this, everyone became comfortable with her dual roles. She gained confidence as an office parent and eventually became an effective full manager of the office.

As Dr. Thomas Gordon notes in *P. E. T. Parent Effectiveness Training,* children do not consider themselves equal in power to their parents. This is not just due to the difference in physical size; it is even true when the teenager is physically bigger than the parents. This is due to a difference in "psychological size" since the parent has powers that are greater than those of the child. These powers can come from punishments that the parents can apply. But if threats are the prime reasons for the difference, the result will be a dysfunctional family. More often, in a healthy family, this difference in psychological size is due to the children's respect and admiration for their parents and their belief that their parents know and understand more. Even when fighting with their parents, children usually have great respect for them. They test their boundaries and, actually, have higher respect for a parent who is strong enough to follow through on policies even under the cajoling and whining of the child.

The same is true in a well-functioning office. Frontline workers must have respect for their managers and consider them to be "bigger" due to their greater knowledge and/or experience. They look to management to protect them from the challenges and threats of the "outside world" just as children look to their parents to protect them from harm. If they begin to believe that their managers do not have their interests at heart or the strength to uphold their convictions, they can rebel in dangerous ways. When employees feel that their managers care about them and are fair and strong, they can accept negative answers to their requests, take them in stride, and still work happily for the good of the company.

Managers must accept the fact that staff members will talk about them behind their backs. This is normal. Children are always getting together to complain about their parents, so managers shouldn't be the least bit surprised (or hurt) when their office family does the same. This is part of what creates the cooperative bond that lets these siblings work together rather than constantly striving to protect their own positions within the family.

Find the Leader of the Group

There is a leader in any group of siblings, just as in any group of people. This might be the oldest sibling (the most experienced employee), but that is not always the case. However, there will always be one member of the group whom the others tend to follow. It is critical for any manager to identify that person and make sure that person is leading the group down the right path.

Phil

In our own office, for many years, we had a very interesting situation. Doris and I were the owners, but we had an office manager, Janice, who ran the day-to-day operations and directly supervised the frontline personnel. We were frequently out of the office, participating in consulting and speaking engagements. When we were in our office, Doris was the de facto emotional or motivational leader of our staff. If staff spirits were dropping, she was able to notice that and pick them up. She could feel the pulse of the staff and bring in some humor or a special treat when it was needed. If frightening things were happening in the economy or industry, she helped the employees feel safe and secure.

However, when Doris was out of the office, Janice, who did an excellent job of managing, was not the "real" emotional leader of the group. Among the frontline siblings, there was a particular individual, Anne, who tended to influence the spirit of the team when Doris was not present. When Anne was in an upbeat mood, she was a very good influence, but when she was down, she could bring down the whole spirit of the office, and problems would develop.

When people are unhappy, they tend to find things to complain about. During some challenging times in the industry, Anne tended to get discouraged more frequently. This would also happen when she was having problems at home. We would come back from a trip and have to spend several days bringing back an upbeat attitude among the staff.

Doris noticed this recurring challenge and decided to attack it proactively. Before leaving for a particular trip, Doris sat down with Anne and told her how impressed she was with her ability to influence the rest of the staff. She told Anne how she had noticed that when she was up, the staff was up, but when she was down, the whole staff reacted similarly. Doris told her why she didn't want the staff to get depressed over what was happening in the industry and why there was no reason for our staff to be concerned. She told Anne that she was counting on her to keep up the spirits of the staff in her absence. When Doris returned from that trip, staff morale was the best it had ever been after such an absence. After that, Doris gave Anne a similar pep talk before each absence of more than a couple of days and the problem was solved. The staff held together against a common enemy—fear of changes in the industry and the temporary lack of emotional leadership due to Doris's absence—when their chosen substitute leader was primed for the task.

"Tell management we've identified the office leader."

It is critical that the manager of an office accept the existence of the "natural" leader of the group. Rather than resenting this, the manager must create an alliance with this chosen leader, so they may work together to guide the rest of the office in positive directions.

One Group of Siblings Ganging Up on Another Sibling

Another scenario that can harm an entire office over time is the cooperation of most or all of the co-workers to gang up on another one.

Phil

Doris and I consulted with an office that was having productivity challenges and low morale. After watching them at work and talking to several of the frontline workers as well as the manager, we determined that most of the group was spending a lot of energy on resenting and finding fault with Jane, one of their co-workers. Jane was a little slower than the rest but was well liked by customers and did her work well. She was very gracious and always willing to help anyone. Although she socialized somewhat with the others, she tended to go her own way. She usually didn't eat lunch with the rest of the staff, who regularly ate together in the lunchroom. Instead, she frequently chose to go out to lunch with her husband, who worked in the area.

Members of the staff were continually reporting unimportant things that she had done and literally looked for things to criticize. They watched the clock to report if she was out of the office a few minutes too long at lunch.

Fortunately, Jane was relatively oblivious to what was happening, but the attitude of her co-workers was negatively impacting the effectiveness of the staff. This was a case of cooperation among siblings against a common enemy, but for the wrong reasons. They had become a cohesive team, but their efforts were spent on proving themselves superior to another member of their ranks, not on achieving success for the company as a whole. Part of the reason the morale was so low was the guilt felt by many of the perpetrators. They felt bad about what was happening and that they were part of it, but they couldn't separate themselves from the majority of their co-workers.

We recommended to management that they needed to get this problem fixed before they could improve the morale and productivity of the staff. We suggested that they hold a staff meeting and discuss in a general way how important it was for everyone to work together. We did not believe it would be helpful to mention the precise problem at this meeting, but they needed to make the staff realize that management knew what was happening and wanted it to stop.

Then, we suggested that they determine who the ringleader was. As noted earlier, there is always a leader in a group. Ringleaders, however, frequently do not even realize they are leading the group. They don't realize they are hurting the one they are picking on, or they at least find comfort that they're not the only ones doing this—"everyone is."

After determining that Grace was the leader (which was quite obvious to us after our observations of the group), the manager sat down with her and discussed the matter. She pointed out how the staff was treating Jane and reminded Grace of some of the wonderful characteristics Jane had and of her willingness to help anyone anytime. Without stating that she knew that Grace was at the core of this treatment, the manager praised Grace's ability to lead her co-workers and requested her help in stopping this mistreatment of Jane. She asked Grace to work with Jane on a cooperative activity to help her gain some speed and efficiency. Grace glowed with the praise and promised to do her best to help. Over the next few weeks, when someone would criticize Jane, Grace became the one who reminded them of something good Jane had done. She had now become Jane's protector. Gradually, as this negative activity stopped and Grace and Jane got to know each other better by working together successfully on the assigned project, the entire staff morale rose and productivity went back to where it should have been.

As this story demonstrates, siblings can work together for positive or negative causes. When they willingly come together, there is usually a positive force in action. However, when peer pressure brings them together, the results can be harmful. Employees who succumb to peer pressure to do something that they know is wrong suffer from feelings of guilt, which interfere with their ability to perform at their best.

Peer pressure in offices is just as strong as it is among children and teenagers. People do not want to be left out or feel alone and will, therefore, frequently join in on activities that they would not do on their own just to remain part of the group. Effective managers are alert to any peer pressure within their office that could be harmful to the overall group.

Safety in Numbers

Doris

Our daughter, Dana, worked at the front desk of a well-known hotel several years ago. The low-level supervisors, although well trained in the technical and operational aspects of their job, had little management or supervisory training. As a result, resentment built up between these entry-level supervisors and the front-desk staff they supervised. However, no one was willing to go to a higher level of management to discuss the situation, for fear of being singled out and then punished in some way for speaking up.

Letting this type of situation continue is not healthy for any company. Higher-level managers were unaware of the frustrations and resentments building among the frontline workers or of the decline in staff morale. Eventually, as will usually happen, an incident occurred to get the frontline employees angry enough to work together and do something about it. A visiting basketball team, staying at the hotel, gave a number of tickets to one of the hotel managers, with the express instructions to please pass them out to the front-desk personnel who had been so helpful to them during their stay. However, the managers decided to use the tickets themselves.

One of the frontline workers got most of the group together and composed a letter to the hotel's general manager about what had been happening, giving this incident as a specific example. The group members each signed the letter, so no one person stood out. Again, this was a case of siblings getting together to try to improve their situation without placing any single individual at high risk, since it would have been difficult to punish or fire the whole group. The note got the attention of the general manager, who met with several of the signers and made some changes. Promising confidentiality, he then held regular meetings with representatives of the front-desk staff to keep things under better control and instituted some management training for the first-level managers.

Clearly, the situation should not have reached this level. If higher-level managers had kept their antennae up, it would not have reached this flashpoint. Unionized employees have a representative they can go to with complaints while remaining anonymous to their bosses. Non-unionized companies should find ways to make it clear to their employees that lower-level people can be comfortable and safe when they identify problems that are affecting the working conditions, productivity, or morale of the staff. Taking care of a problem before it explodes will always be better than cleaning up the damage later. Regular staff meetings, or, in offices with large numbers of frontline people, focus groups, where people have the opportunity to safely air minor gripes can frequently prevent such situations from escalating. A place where employees can anonymously leave comments about problems can also help to bring out important information on what is happening before a crisis develops. In addition, since these are the people who perform the repetitive daily tasks, the company will gain important advice on how to improve current policies, increase productivity, and/or reduce costs. Employees whose opinions are sought and implemented when appropriate will have better morale and will work harder than those who continually resent their management.

Helping Siblings Work as a Team

With proper management, siblings can be encouraged to work together as a team. Management must constantly be on the lookout for when siblings are either not working as a team or are cooperating in harmful ways. Set up teams to work on projects. Have strong leaders mentor weaker siblings. Put co-workers who might otherwise fight with each other on one team. Give them goals to reach for. If they don't work together, they will both fail. In most cases, this will force them to cooperate and get the job done.

Positive peer pressure can be a great motivator. However, don't give them the assignment and sit back thinking everything is under control. Keep track to make sure they are working together and not continually bickering or competing with each other. Praise their mutual successes, not just their individual ones. If one of the team comes to complain, don't interfere. Let them work it out together. Remind them of the objectives you have assigned and let them know that you want to see the results, not every petty problem encountered.

A form of management popularized by Tom Peters and known as "MBWA"—or "Management by Walking Around"—is very sound. Only by mingling with employees can a manager get a real feeling of what is happening. If a manager waits until someone else brings a problem to the surface, the damage may be far too advanced to fix.

External Challenges

In these days, throughout our economy, workers feel stressed and uneasy. Downsizing and mergers occur even in good economic times, so people don't feel secure in their jobs. This environment can create a greater sense of competition among co-workers, who are protecting their turf. If management is sensitive to these concerns, however, they can turn the tendency of a group to cooperate against a common enemy to the company's advantage, and make the workplace a less competitive and stressful place for everyone. Managers should find ways, sometimes with humor, to remind employees that the enemy is outside; it is not each other. If they all work together, the team will succeed and remain intact. With the continual closing of businesses, mergers, and other consolidations, it is important to keep a family spirit within the office to maintain high morale and keep everyone working together at their highest levels.

Doris

From our earliest times of owning a business, we tried to provide opportunities for the staff to get together outside the office socially. We had a pool in our backyard, so each summer we would invite our employees to bring their spouses, significant other if there was one, and children to a pool party. In the winter, we would go out together at company expense for a holiday dinner right before Christmas. In the early years, we could only afford to host the employees themselves, but in later years, we encouraged them to bring their spouses.

For many years, we have closed the office one Friday each year and taken the staff on a weekend trip. Such activities provide opportunities to get to know each other better in a friendly, unpressured atmosphere and can create excellent bonding.

Many companies provide picnics, dinners, and even trips to their employees for such bonding purposes. The results of greater friendship and cooperation lead to greater productivity, which more than pays for the cost of the event.

Remember, as a manager, you will sometimes be the common enemy. This is not necessarily bad unless you take it personally. If you do take it personally, you will set the scene for an "us vs. them" conflict. This is never healthy for any family. There has to be a basic respect of the children for their parents even if they sometimes believe that their parents aren't right. And parents must accept the fact that their children will sometimes resent them, even if they have tried to be scrupulously fair. Ignore these challenges and continue making decisions that you honestly consider to be fair, reasonable, and best for everyone's common interests. This type of management will maximize a spirit among the troops to work together for the common good.

If you don't understand how a woman could both love her sister dearly and want to wring her neck at the same time, then you were probably an only child.
—Linda Sunshine
Mom Loves Me Best
(And Other Lies You Told Your Sister)

Tips from Managers

1. Develop a tougher skin—no matter what you do, they *will* talk about you behind your back.

2. Practice MBWA—walk around your office with your antennae raised.

3. Be sensitive to situations where several employees are ganging up against another one.

4. Create projects and situations where you can encourage teamwork.

5. Create incentives for the team as a whole to bring out a cooperative spirit.

6. Understand exactly who is the leader of the group and make that person your ally.

7. Expect employees to test their boundaries, and be fair and strong in your responses to such tests.

8. Listen with an open mind to questions or complaints brought to your attention by employees. They know what is happening within the group and are aware of things you are not.

9. Set up regular staff meetings or focus groups where you ask questions and listen more than you speak. This will help you know what is happening and give you good ideas on improving current procedures and policies.

10. Understand that your employees will be concerned about anything they feel can affect the security of their jobs. This can be matters within the company as well as things they read in the newspapers. Be aware of company, industry, and national conditions that might foster anxiety in your employees and discuss these openly with them.

Tips from Employees

1. Seek our good characteristics; don't always look for our faults.

2. Find ways in which we can work cooperatively with our peers.

3. Make sure that decisions you make are for the good of our whole office, not just for one or two of us.

4. Help direct the leaders among us whom we tend to follow.

5. When you see some of our co-workers starting to team up in negative ways, please try to stop it.

6. Help us feel safe in coming to you with a problem. Otherwise, we'll be afraid to and you may not know what is happening until it is too late.

7. Talk to us about what is happening in our company or industry so we don't have to believe the "grapevine" or rumor mill.

8. Hold staff meetings or focus groups where we can be honest without fear. Provide a place where we can let you know what is happening without identifying ourselves.

9. Keep your eyes and ears tuned to our grapevine so you can know what is happening. Don't just stay in your own office.

10. Help all of us to do our best and to work together on behalf of our entire group.

CHAPTER 3

The Oldest Child:
Who's Really in Charge?

Age is something that doesn't matter, unless you are a cheese.

—Billie Burke

Doris and Phil

Many years ago, we owned a branch office with a staff of four people, a manager and three employees. The manager's husband was taking a new position with his company that would require their moving out of our area, so she had to resign her position.

Not being very experienced in business at that time, we automatically promoted our most senior employee, Roberta, to the position of manager. She had been an excellent travel agent who got along very well with her co-workers and clients. However, we quickly realized that Roberta had no supervisory skills and, although respected as a travel agent by her co-workers, was earning no respect as a manager. The agency was deteriorating quickly, both in morale and productivity.

Since neither of us was in a position to go down and run the branch on a long-term basis, we had a problem. We tried to train Roberta, but, possibly because she was already nearing retirement age, she was either unable or unwilling to learn major new skills. In fact, due to her somewhat dysfunctional relationships with her adult son and daughter, we should have realized that her supervisory skills were minimal.

Ultimately, because of our poor decision to promote her based solely on her seniority, our only choice was to fire Roberta and bring in an outside, new employee to manage the branch. We lost a good travel agent and had to work very hard to repair the damage created by our mistake. This was one of the times that taught us clearly that seniority is not an adequate reason for a promotion that requires new and different skills.

When Mom and Dad are out for the evening, who is usually in charge? Isn't the oldest child (if old enough to do so) usually asked to babysit for siblings? When the manager of an office is away, isn't the most senior subordinate automatically put in charge of the rest of the staff? In fact, aren't both of these scenarios the norm even when the oldest or most senior is not the most capable one for the job? Even if they have had no training about being a supervisor?

The special position and rights of the oldest child has been part of Western culture from biblical times. Primogeniture, the rule of inheritance whereby real property such as land and buildings went to the oldest son, if a man died without a will, was the law in ancient Israel, throughout medieval Europe, and within most Western cultures. Even in the United States, the rule of primogeniture only started to change after the Revolutionary War.

Labor unions, in effect, continued this type of policy as they gained strength within the American business world. Promotions, salaries, and protection against layoffs in bad times were based on seniority, or length of employment, rather than merit. Even today, there are many employee contracts that base such things on who has been there the longest, making them, in effect, the "oldest" children.

In today's offices, the oldest child may not be the one who has lived the most years but who has worked for the company the longest. Even now, we tend to promote the most senior employee and expect this person to take home the highest salary. However, this is frequently unfair to junior members of the staff and can be quite detrimental to the efficiency and profitability of the business as a whole.

Second in Command by Default

In many homes and offices, the oldest child becomes the second in command to the parents merely by default. This method of choosing leadership can lead to very dysfunctional families or businesses. When a more senior employee without management skills is allowed or even encouraged to "boss around" a less senior but more capable employee, dissatisfaction quickly occurs in the "younger" employee. The company will soon find itself with the older employee still on the job and the younger, very capable, and promising employee resigning.

Just as the oldest child in a family is not always the best suited to rule over the younger members, the most senior employee is not always the one deserving the highest salary or the best one to choose for positions of leadership. Management must stay in touch with people's actual abilities and their aspirations. Then, they need to make sure that everyone knows who is in charge when the manager is not available. By not structuring a chain of command, things are left to chance and chaos is usually the result. Resentments will fester and erupt, affecting the relationships in the office, even when the manager is present.

Some people are ready for additional responsibilities earlier than others, and some will never be ready for such assignments. There are no realistic, meaningful rules or even guidelines for how much experience a person should have or how old they should be in order to take on managerial-level functions.

In our family, Donald, from the time he was ten, was quite capable of short babysitting responsibilities with his younger sister and brother. By the time he was thirteen, he could even make dinner for them. He was more responsible than many of our fourteen- to sixteen-year-old babysitters. The only thing he couldn't do was drive them to soccer, gymnastics, or other activities.

Doris had a similar experience many years ago when our business was still quite young. However, in this case, it was not the oldest member of the staff who demonstrated such obvious management capability.

Doris

Due to growth, we needed to expand our staff by one person and were fortunate to find a very capable yet inexperienced person for the position. The staff, at that time, consisted of myself as manager and Sara and Susan, two frontline, good-quality employees. Within just a few months, Barbara, the new person, showed a potential for leadership that was quickly obvious to me.

If I was away from the office, Sara and Susan would seek Barbara's advice when they were unsure of something. By the end of Barbara's first year with us, I had earmarked her as a prospective manager for our office. As Barbara neared the end of her second year, I named her office manager, allowing me to concentrate on administrative and marketing functions rather than on day-to-day management details. She continued in that position for more than twenty years.

Sara and Susan, our two "older" employees, who had seniority over Barbara, were both quite satisfied with this choice, since they knew that she was the right person for the job and the lines of communication were kept open. They had almost chosen Barbara themselves by going to her for management assistance when I was not there.

If one of the older employees had wanted to be manager, it might not have been the right choice for the overall office. Sometimes a manager has to be firm and select the person who is best for the job. It is important, however, to make sure that senior employees do not feel slighted or inferior. Praise their abilities. And tell them you trust them to work with the younger or less senior person who is now in charge of the office or the specific project.

Teenager in the Office

Sometimes an employee gets burned out. We're sure you've seen it before; an employee (very often one of your senior employees) starts getting brash and lazy and begins to misbehave. Several times every year, magazines like *Time* and *Newsweek* and metropolitan newspapers run cover or major stories on "Stress in the Workplace." Being burned out is almost a badge of honor in our society today.

One of the symptoms of the burned-out employee is behavior similar to that of a teenager. This type of employee may be impertinent and rebellious and may continually test the rules of the company. He or she may even be defiant when questioned about an action (or lack thereof).

Just as a teenager can stress and disrupt an entire family, such an employee causes the same dysfunction within an office. This person tries to get out of doing "grunge" work and feels above the rules. Co-workers notice such actions and either resent or try to emulate them. Either way, the office has problems that interfere with both morale and productivity.

There are several ways of handling such employees. Wherever possible, try to let them work on their own on a project that needs their experience and expertise. When properly challenged with such a meaningful project, many employees forget their rebelliousness and get involved and dedicated to the project. In such cases, the problem tends to resolve itself without acrimony or disruptions.

Unfortunately, not all teenagers can be distracted from their defiance. In such cases, managers might have to take the employee aside privately to discuss the problem. It is best, though, not to confront head-on. Instead of telling such employees that they are not following the rules or pulling their weight, it is much better to remark that you have noticed that the employee seems to be feeling under pressure and getting burned out. People don't get insulted when someone tells them they are acting stressed or burned out. In many cases, they will eagerly agree with this assessment.

Doris and Phil

Sally, who had been a model employee and very productive for many years, had begun acting like a typical teenager. Her work quality had declined and she was always finding things to complain about, creating negative attitudes among her co-workers. When we talked to her about being burned out, she readily agreed. We suggested that perhaps she should take some time off, get rested, and then decide if she wanted to come back or not. Maybe she was getting unhappy with the industry and its challenges and wanted to do something different.

Sally did not need the income from her job and we were entering our slow season, so we didn't have to replace her immediately. She was very happy to be offered an opportunity to take some time off. She had not real-ized that her actions were affecting the entire office and would not have approached us to request time off, fearing that it would be an irreversible choice. We told her that we would get in touch with her before filling her position to see if she wanted to come back.

As it turned out, when we decided to fill the position after about three months, she decided not to return. However, a little more than a year later, she learned that we had an opening and called to see if she could come back. After trying some other things, she found that she missed the travel industry and wanted to return and work for us. We invited her back and she remained with us for several more years before retiring for good. During her absence, the morale in the office was excellent and, when she returned, her attitude had changed and she again became an asset. It's very much like what happens after a teenager grows up and becomes a productive member of the family again.

You won't find that the above solution can work in all cases, since not everyone has the luxury of taking time off and might be afraid to quit and try to find another job. If this is the case, you should make these employees aware of the effect their attitude and/or behavior is having on other staff members. They and you must realize that their attitude will have to change or they should find a new job where they will be happier. In extreme cases, it might even be necessary to fire such a person, in spite of their longevity. However, because of their time with the company, it is critical to give them as much assistance as possible to solve the problems. If you jump too quickly to forcing them out, you may very well demoralize the rest of the staff. Perhaps, through an open dialogue, you could come up with some specific problems that are causing the burnout, such as working too much overtime, not taking lunch breaks or vacations, etc. It may even just be that they are taking their current job for granted and believing that the grass has to be greener somewhere else. If you are able to find a cause, you and the employee can work together toward correcting it.

Another type of teenage behavior that must not be allowed is insubordination. When a frontline employee tells a supervisor "you are wrong" in front of other staff members, the situation must be handled firmly and quickly. We had an experience many years ago involving this type of situation.

Doris and Phil

Our senior frontline staff member, Cynthia, went to a seminar to learn how to compute prices for a complex sale. After she returned, she had to figure one of these prices and bring it to Doris for approval. Cynthia failed to follow an important price-construction rule. When her supervisor, Mary, advised her of her error, Cynthia shouted in front of the rest of the staff, "You're wrong! This is what I was taught in class yesterday." It was obvious to her supervisor that Cynthia had either misunderstood her instructor or the instructor had made an error.

When Mary tried to show Cynthia the rule, she wouldn't listen and shouted, "You think you know everything!" At that point, Cynthia was out of control and not ready or able to accept any kind of instruction. The rest of the staff was shocked.

Mary sternly told Cynthia to go home and not return until she had gained control of herself. (This is akin to sending a defiant child to her room to calm down.)

About two hours later, Cynthia called Mary, apologized for her actions, and was invited to return to the office the next morning. At that time, Mary showed Cynthia the rule, which made it clear that Cynthia had incorrectly interpreted what was said in class.

Had Mary tried to continue the discussion with Cynthia instead of removing her from the office, the situation would have only deteriorated. When an employee becomes irrational, the only appropriate action is removal from the office until rationality returns.

Mary's action in removing Cynthia was the best choice whether or not Cynthia was correct about the facts. Once Cynthia left the office, Mary checked out the rule and found she, herself, was correct. Had Mary discovered she was wrong, she should have been willing, once Cynthia apologized for her disrespectful actions, to admit her error and discuss the rule with Cynthia. She should then have pointed out to Cynthia that she was not exiled from the office because she had disagreed with Mary; it was because of the insubordinate manner in which she had disagreed. A parent should never be afraid to admit to a mistake, but cannot let the child be rude and insubordinate in pointing out the error.

Even an Experienced Employee Can Grow

If you want to keep your experienced longtime employees content and productive in their job, it is important to provide opportunities for them to continue to grow. Just as teenagers hate boredom, so do employees. Studies have proven that people become dissatisfied with their jobs when they feel everything is the same and there is nothing new to learn.

As your older, more experienced employees gain more experience, make sure that you keep challenging their skills to create such growth. Your more experienced people should not be doing the same tasks as less experienced staff members. Obviously, when there is a crisis, everyone should help out without regard for whether or not a task is "beneath" their skill level. But in the normal course of business, experienced (and probably higher paid) employees should be doing the tasks that demand their skill levels while newer, less experienced workers focus on tasks most appropriate to their skill levels. This way, everyone is on a continual learning path—neither overwhelmed by tasks beyond their capabilities nor bored by functions that anyone could do.

Do Not Take Unfair Advantage of Your Oldest Child

There is another side to this coin, however. Parents have a tendency to take advantage of their oldest child by requiring "babysitting" of the younger children without compensation, even in cases where they know the older child has other plans. This requires the oldest child to take on responsibilities normally expected of parents (giving up other plans because the children need you), and is not a fair expectation without compensation for the sacrifice.

Although your senior employees can be great helpers in mentoring newer employees, they should be appreciated for these beyond-call activities. If they are paid based on commissions, this should be taken into account if they are asked to spend time away from selling. Since they cannot earn commissions while they are helping a newer co-worker, they should be paid extra to make up for the commission they will lose during this time.

We were involved in two situations that illustrate this concept—one in a friend's family and one in an office.

Doris

A teenage daughter of a friend of ours was the oldest in a large family. Connie always appeared to be very self-confident and mature. She frequently volunteered to help out with her younger siblings. Her mother, with the responsibility for seven other children, tended to depend on Connie as almost a second mother. She greatly appreciated Connie's help but, with all the pressures on her, forgot to let Connie know how much. She just assumed that Connie knew how proud and grateful she was.

One day, without any notice, Connie ran away from home. Luckily, she called us to let us know she was OK and asked us to call and tell her mother. She spilled her heart out to us, telling us how she always had to do so much more than her siblings but how no one appreciated her. She really believed that her mother loved her siblings more and that she was living a "Cinderella" life. Everything had been blown up out of proportion, but her perception was what mattered.

When we called her mother to report that she was safe, we told her mother the gist of what she had said to us. Her mother was absolutely shocked! She admitted that she actually felt closer to Connie than to any of her other children since Connie was always so willing to help out and was so mature. She had never realized Connie's need to be told how much she was loved and appreciated.

Having spoken to both of them and having heard both sides of what was happening, we were able to bring them together. They began to communicate better and Connie's mother made sure to show appreciation for Connie's help and not abuse it.

Doug was consulting with a company that was having a major employee-morale challenge in one of their offices, based on a similar situation.

Doug

The manager of the office was out on a three-month maternity leave and the senior employee, Jeanne, was automatically expected to pick up the slack. Jeanne was not being paid anything additional for this work. This was a typical situation anytime the manager was out, but this longer absence was creating major resentment in Jeanne and was affecting the morale and effectiveness of the entire office.

I recommended to the company management that there were two fair choices in this type of situation. What they were doing was unfair to Jeanne and destined to create resentment, which could even result in Jeanne's resignation (a form of running away in the business world) if it was not corrected. Jeanne was feeling unappreciated and abused and there was merit to her perception.

I suggested that one valid choice to restore fairness was to compensate Jeanne anytime managerial duties were added to her normal workload for more than a couple of days. The other choice was to assign some of her usual work to the rest of the staff during such managerial absences so her overall workload would not change. In either event, she should be told clearly and publicly how much her help during this period was appreciated so that she could know that she was not being taken for granted.

Untrained Supervisors Are Like Bossy Older Siblings

One of the biggest complaints of frontline workers is to be under the command, even if only temporarily, of a co-worker who suddenly, with this additional authority, acts "bossy."

When senior employees are even temporarily assigned managerial duties, they should be at least minimally trained on supervisory skills. They must be helped to realize that this is a temporary position of authority and that they will return to a more equal co-worker status when it ends. It is important for them to retain a friendly and cooperative relationship with their co-workers. People placed in such temporary positions tend to try to enforce every little policy, sometimes just to show that they are in control. They have to be taught not to "sweat the small stuff." Otherwise, they can abuse their power and create situations that result in long-term resentments within the office.

Don't Forget the Younger Children

As we work to help focus our most experienced employees on the most challenging tasks, we can't forget our younger, newer workers. They must remain challenged as well. They can become very resentful if they perceive that the exciting or challenging tasks are always given to the oldest one. This is no different from the complaint at home that "he always gets to stay up later than me" or "she's allowed to cross the street alone—why can't I?"

*"Seniority doesn't mean you can giggle
during my presentation, Dave."*

If managers do not make sure to encourage the growth of all workers, they will lose younger, less experienced, but potentially very valuable employees. Managing personnel fairly and taking care to distribute all tasks are distributed equitably, based on a variety of factors including seniority, is a full-time activity. One of the worst things a manager can do is blindly hand out assignments based on seniority alone.

The older I grow, the more I distrust the familiar doctrine that age brings wisdom.   —H. L. Mencken

Tips from Managers

1. Acknowledge the greater abilities of your more experienced employees.

2. Provide opportunities to all employees that will allow them to develop in their jobs.

3. Keep your antennae up for signs of boredom on the job from your experienced employees.

4. Let your experienced employees mentor your newer people and help them grow.

5. Acknowledge that more senior employees can have some additional privileges over newer ones, but be careful not to go so far that the newer ones resent the differences. Remember that seniority does count for something, but so does merit. Stay in balance.

6. Remember to praise those experienced employees—don't take them for granted.

7. Provide training opportunities, both in the office and by sending employees to outside sources, that will help them feel they are growing in their jobs.

8. Seek suggestions and opinions from experienced employees when you are making decisions on changes. This will make them feel important and needed.

9. When you have an employee who is acting like a teenager but who is otherwise a very valuable employee, try to structure that person's job so they can work alone on projects to reduce their negative effect on others.

10. Do not let a rebellious or defiant employee control you; others in the office will be uncomfortable and will not respect you for allowing it to happen.

Tips from Employees

1. Please reward us when we are working harder or producing more than our co-workers, even if they have been here longer.

2. Be reasonable about your requests of us. Don't automatically give all the "plum" tasks to the most senior employee. When a junior employee can do the job just as well or better, please consider this.

3. Give each of us a fair chance to earn promotions and to grow in our jobs.

4. Do not be intimidated by employees who defy you; it is your job to make sure they do what they are supposed to do. We respect you when you control the situation with fairness; we don't respect you when you allow one of us to walk all over you.

5. If we seem to be getting "burned out," please try to help us get re-motivated. If we are having a specific problem where our job is impacting negatively on our family, try to work with us to correct it.

6. Do not be afraid to fire a senior employee if you cannot either get them to work as part of the team or find a solo function that they can do away from the rest of us.

7. Please remember not to take us for granted just because we've been here for years. We still need to be exposed to new and interesting tasks and ideas.

8. Do not take advantage of us when we are the senior employee by piling every tough job on us because we're the "best" one to handle it. Let some of our co-workers learn how to do these as well so that we have a fair workload, not a crushing one.

9. When you promote one of us to a supervisory position, please be sure that the person you are promoting is capable of supervising people without demoralizing them.

10. When you promote someone to a supervisory position, please provide them with relationship and personnel management training, not just the technical training they need for their new position.

CHAPTER 4

The Baby of the Family:
Let Me Stand on My Own Feet!

For years we have given scientific attention to the care and rearing of plants and animals, but we have allowed babies to be raised chiefly by tradition.
—Edith Belle Lowry
False Modesty

Doug

In my early twenties, I was an independent contractor covering a sales territory for a major car-rental company. I had grown up in the travel industry, so I knew the market. The area had been underserved previously, and I was able to more than double sales in the territory in my first year.

As the area grew, the company brought in a new manager, and I began to discuss transitioning from an independent contractor to a full employee with benefits. At the same time, a major competitor had heard about my success and contacted me about coming to work for them. I had no real desire to leave and go to the other company since I felt loyal to my current company for their original willingness to hire me at such a young age.

I met with my boss about becoming an employee and expressed some disappointment at the slow pace of movement. Meanwhile, I interviewed with the other company but still expected things to work out with the first. When the offer to be an employee with my original company finally came in, I was surprised to find that they intended to split my territory into three territories and give me only one-third of my original area. Since a significant portion of my compensation was based on a sales incentive, this hurt my wallet and my pride. I believed I should keep the entire area and continue to build it. In spite of my success to date, my new boss told me, "Doug, you have to take things slowly and walk before you run."

I was bothered by her unwillingness to let me grow after I had already demonstrated my ability to perform. The competitor, on the other hand, was willing to look past my age and hired me as their youngest regional sales manager. I was very happy and productive in that job and only left when the opportunity to grow and run my own sales force presented itself.

The baby of the family. It conjures up images. Five-year-old Susie being watched out for by her bigger brothers and sisters. Ten-year-old Susie trying to be like her bigger brothers and sisters. Forty-year-old Susan, the professional and mother of three teenagers, who is still the "baby" at family reunions!

While the turnover in a typical office usually means that no one is the "baby" of the "office family" for too long, the fact is that every office has its newcomers and its veterans. Some offices with very stable staff have established positions in the pecking order for many years. How managers recognize and react to their newer employees often affects much more than merely that individual's performance—it can affect the entire team.

In our experience at our own offices and in helping other managers run their offices better, we have found that most situations of this type can be discussed across two dimensions: (1) the desire of the employee and (2) the perception and intent of the manager. The former refers to the desire "babies of the office family" have to grow; the latter refers to how prepared managers think the "baby" is to take on additional responsibility and/or how willing they are to push them to take additional responsibility. The result is four general scenarios.

Employee Desires to Grow. Manager Doesn't Allow Growth.	Employee Doesn't Want to Grow. Manager Doesn't Want Growth.
Employee Desires to Grow. Manager Encourages Growth.	Employee Doesn't Want to Grow. Manager Wants Growth.

Employee Desires to Grow/ Manager Doesn't Allow Growth

In one type of situation, babies of offices are clamoring to grow, but managers don't think they are as ready as they think they are. In some cases, these managers are traditionally assessing the job maturity of their "babies." Our home families are full of examples where the youngest child wants to be like the older kids but just isn't ready. In many cases, however, these managers are projecting their past experience onto newer employees or simply assuming that, due to their shorter time in the office, they can't possibly be ready. They don't really want them to be ready because it diminishes the importance of the manager's role in continuing to rule them. Any parents who have had children beyond a few years old remember the combination of joy and sadness and perhaps a bit of apprehension as they suddenly realized their once-dependent children were perfectly capable of doing something on their own.

"Ted would like to know how long he'll be the 'new' employee."

Donald

When I graduated from college and joined the air force, I was assigned to the Ballistic Missile Office (BMO). I was given the responsibility to put together a very large "request for proposal" (RFP) for a source selection. RFPs are how the air force asks companies for bids on a project, and source selections are how they evaluate the proposals they receive to pick the winner(s).

In recognition of how well I had prepared the RFP (obviously with a lot of help from others), my boss chose me to serve on the evaluation committee for the source selection. This is the group of people who review all of the team's individual expert evaluations and prepare the official evaluation for

the general, who will make the selection. The evaluation committee is usu-
ally made up exclusively of captains, majors, and higher-ranking officers.
Selecting a second lieutenant was unusual. Therein lay the honor, and the
foundation of what later would be a challenge for me.

After the thirty-day initial review period by the full team, the evalua-
tion committee began to meet. My immediate boss, a captain, was away
for the first two days, and the committee was led by the lieutenant colonel
who chose me to be on the team.

As the meetings went on, I felt that all of my ideas were being given lit-
tle real consideration, even when it was in the particular area of my
expertise. On the one hand, I was grateful that I had been given the
opportunity to participate at a higher level than most junior officers, but
on the other hand, I was quickly feeling as though I was being treated as
the baby of the group.

On the third day, the treatment became obvious. My immediate boss, the
captain, returned from his trip and joined the deliberations. He immediately
questioned several of the interim analyses with virtually the same logic I had
tried but failed with during the preceding two days. The "elder brother's"
logic carried the day while the "baby's" logic was summarily dismissed.
Rather than fume, I decided to address the issue directly with my lieutenant
colonel. I told him that it seemed as though I was being viewed as "the kid"
and the general attitude was that "there was no way that 'the kid's' opinion
could really be valid and he ought to be glad just to be there." I pointed out
that, while I was honored with the selection, it was of limited value if my
opinion would never be heard. The lieutenant colonel smiled and admitted
that such descriptions had been used by other committee members. He apol-
ogized for going along with the flow and promised to make sure that every-
one had an equal say. He really didn't want to prevent anyone's willingness
to grow, "baby" or not; and from then on, I thoroughly enjoyed my oppor-
tunity to contribute.

This is in contrast to the experience Doug had in the story that started
this chapter.

It is very easy to fall into the trap of underestimating new employees,
assuming that as the babies of the office they can't possibly be ready for
a full load.

Phil

When our travel agency was just a few years old, we hired a new per-
son to join our staff of four. Although not the youngest person in the office

in terms of chronological age, she was, of course, new to our company and our industry and was, therefore, the "baby" of our office. As is customarily done with babies and young children, our manager and the other employees worked hard to train and help her.

However, we didn't realize that we were going too far in our helping our newest sibling. Instead of letting her develop to be independent in her work, one or another employee kept doing the work for her to show her how. We only realized what we were doing when she rebelled and let us know that she wanted to do it herself. This was very similar to the young child who declares, "I want to do it myself." Fortunately, we realized that we were being overhelpful. We began letting her loose to work on her own, knowing she could come to us if she needed help. She grew in the job and became very adept at the work. This experience taught us to encourage new employees to work on their own as quickly as they were able to do so—a strategy that has served us well ever since.

*"I am NOT too 'hands on' as a manager! Now sit
down and let me cut your food for you!"*

Employee Desires to Grow/
Manager Encourages Growth

In many cases, well-developed and secure managers encourage newer and younger employees to grow as fast as they possibly can. They look for opportunities to allow them to develop their skills. They may provide a safety net to ensure against a disaster, but they understand that learning sometimes requires mistakes. Small but embarrassing failures are often life's best lessons.

In the examples with Donald and Doug above, they experienced the limitations when a manager doesn't know how to handle the "baby" of the office family who wants to grow. The big difference, of course, is that Donald's boss had initially offered growth opportunity through the appointment to the source selection evaluation committee and eventually realized his mistake in handling the evaluation process. He adjusted his position to mutual satisfaction and really deserves credit for creating a situation that ultimately allowed Donald to grow, but he had the safety net of the group environment to protect him as well. In Doug's case, there was no satisfaction and his manager's mishandling of this classic office family situation led to the company's loss of a very productive employee.

There are, of course, many different ways for a manager to deal with young or new employees who want to grow. Even when the "baby" in question is less driven than Donald and Doug were, there are opportunities to put successful office parenting techniques to work. The key to success with the baby of the family at home is to protect the child but give them opportunities to grow. It's no different with the office family.

We were able to put this theory to the test in our own office.

Donald

For the first two years of one of our businesses, my assistant was my wife, Yvonne. When she had a baby and decided to stay home, we replaced her with a new, relatively inexperienced individual. At first, I was very frustrated at her seeming inability to do tasks that had been easy for Yvonne. Since the new employee was nervous about replacing my wife, it only compounded the problem.

Then it dawned on me that Yvonne had grown into the job from the start and really was an older member of the office family. Now we were throwing everything at the new person, the "baby," and expecting her to be as good as the older sibling. I met with her and explained that we realized what we had been doing. By taking the pressure off, we gave her a more protected environment. Then, we carefully added one new task at a time. Within several weeks, she was performing at least 80 percent as well as Yvonne had; within a few months, she was up to full speed. Not only did we have a productive employee, but she felt the pride that comes from successful growth.

We would never expect a baby's first words to be "please get me a glass of water, Mommy." We are thrilled with "ma-ma" or "wa-wa." We expect them to learn gradually—the old cliché—crawl before you walk. We should expect the same from new employees.

Employee Doesn't Want to Grow/
Manager Doesn't Want Growth

This is obviously the worst possible combination when it comes to the growth and performance of the individual and office. There are a variety of negative consequences from such a dysfunctional situation. Not only will the baby not grow into a productive sibling in the office, but other officemates can get resentful and demoralized that such a situation is allowed to continue. They expect the office parent to eventually hold everyone to the same standards.

Phil

One business we consulted with had a particularly challenging situation. The owner owned two offices and personally managed one. In the other, she had named her top-producing salesperson the office manager a few years earlier. This manager was a good salesperson but was generally ill prepared to supervise a staff.

As the office grew from just two employees to a full complement of five, certain weaknesses became apparent. Among them was an inability to deal with new employees. The owner had contacted us because the office she managed performed well, but there always seemed to be problems at the other office. She thought that the problems would go away as the office grew, but the more the office grew, the more the problems grew as well. It was getting to a point where her office was suffering from the time she spent fighting fires. The owner, Stephanie, had us meet with the manager of this office, Jen.

Among the problems we found was a new employee who wasn't pulling her weight. After an appropriate ramping-up period, the employee was still meeting a novice's standard at best and seemed to brush off her mistakes as if she shouldn't be expected to know any better. Stephanie was aware of the situation, but she was afraid to push Jen to take action. Jen didn't take criticism all that well, and Stephanie didn't want to risk losing her by putting on too much pressure. Jen, on the other hand, clearly didn't know what to do with this employee and was unwilling take a proactive role to change anything.

To us, it was a classic case of the "parent" (Jen) abdicating her responsibility to help the "baby" (the new employee) to mature. Stephanie was enabling all this by refusing to help build Jen's ability as a manager. We advised Stephanie that, although we understood Jen's value as a salesperson in addition to being the manager, she couldn't let this situation go on.

We told her to either counsel Jen on how to grow as a manager or find a way to move Jen into a pure sales position and away from managerial responsibilities.

Stephanie was afraid to confront Jen or suggest a move that she feared Jen would view as a demotion. Ultimately, however, Stephanie bore more than the pain of potentially losing Jen. Her second-best salesperson was so frustrated with the low morale that she left. The new employee who caused all the pain left shortly thereafter. Jen, citing a desire to take it a little bit easier, resigned a few weeks after that. After a few weeks of "retirement," she ended up working at a competitor as a part-time salesperson.

Not every situation has this unhappy an ending, but allowing newcomers to continue to act as though they are the baby and therefore immune from the need to grow and mature virtually never has a good outcome.

Employee Doesn't Want to Grow/ Manager Wants Growth

Ideally, through good employee recruiting, managers won't find themselves in this situation. But people being people, it's sure to happen to you if you run an office for very long. When encountering a person like this, the important thing is to be supportive, but firm.

Parents who coddle babies inevitably end up with very dependent adults who are unable to fend for themselves and often come running back to Mommy and Daddy for money or whatever else is needed to bail them out of trouble. Unfortunately, sometimes this plays out at work as well.

Donald
We'll never forget one particular employee. She was very bright and interviewed well. Only later did we learn that she demonstrated a pattern of unwillingness to grow beyond being the newcomer. Originally, she did fine, doing reasonable work for being new and making the kinds of mistakes you'd expect of a novice. As time passed, it seemed as though she wasn't improving. We'd counsel her, and like the child who responds for a day or two after being called to task for something by a parent, she would begin to improve.

As soon as the immediate pressure was off, however, she reverted to her novice ways. The biggest frustration for us was that, much like a young kid, she was unwilling to take responsibility for her actions. She was always seeking to lay the blame elsewhere, claim ignorance, or otherwise deflect attention from her own accountability. She was charismatic and knew it, and used her charisma to gain sympathy. To make matters worse, just as with Jen's new agent in the earlier story, her attitude was beginning to have a negative impact on office morale.

Unlike Jen's situation, we were armed with the knowledge of how to handle this case. At first we tried simple counseling, but, frankly, it didn't work. This wasn't much of a surprise since counseling alone often doesn't work with children either. Most people don't respond unless there are known consequences to their actions, so we began a very simple, planned program to hold her specifically accountable for each task—to literally baby her along. We reasoned that she would either (a) improve her performance and attitude (we knew she was capable) or (b) get frustrated by being under the microscope so much and quit (this is one place we can take advantage of not being a true family since you can't get a child to quit your family). We'd like to say it worked out with option "a," but the truth is that about three weeks into our process, she quit over our mild reaction to a somewhat minor mistake. It was obviously the straw that broke the proverbial camel's back. Despite the less-than-perfect outcome, we were still better off than if we had allowed the situation to continue.

Obviously, through good recruiting, a manager can avoid having to deal with a new employee who doesn't want to grow. However, in a large company you may not have the option of choosing all your team members, or you may make a hiring mistake as we did. Either way, it's best to use proven office parenting techniques to get the unwilling "baby" to grow up or opt out.

A Fifth Scenario

There's actually a fifth scenario outside those discussed. What happens when the baby of the family doesn't recognize their position? This situation is so well known that most family sitcoms present shows where the younger sibling tries to be just as big as their bigger brother or sister. From *Leave It to Beaver* to *The Brady Bunch* to *The Cosby Show*, the theme plays through. And we've seen it in the office as well.

Donald

I remember once, at an engineering company I worked in, we had a new employee right out of graduate school. He was very smart and had a lot of book learning, but he had very little direct experience in what we did. He was the "baby" in our family, but unfortunately he didn't realize it.

His ego was obviously large, and he couldn't accept that he was junior and needed first to learn from others. Right from the beginning, he was challenging everyone about how we did things and asserting that he had a better way. If he had ten or twenty years of experience, people may have reacted differently; or if he approached things more from a "help me understand why it's done this way" instead of a "why in the world would you do it that way?" style, people would have accepted his ideas. Instead, he simply ticked everybody off and got frustrated himself. It wasn't long before he found another opportunity. Despite his obvious intelligence, there was no one at this company who was sad to see him go.

Don't Forget the Rest of the Family

Caring for the baby of the office family isn't the only thing an office parent needs to worry about. The arrival of a new office family member can have a profound effect on others within the office. Some of this was covered in the chapter on sibling rivalry, but a few points are worth noting here as well.

1. The arrival of a new member draws attention away from other office members. In families, young children often struggle with a sense of lost identity after a new arrival, because they are no longer the center of attention. Similarly, employees often feel slighted by the perceived reduced attention that comes with no longer being the "baby" in the office family.

2. The arrival of a new member can provoke petty jealousies in other officemates. In families, middle children often tattle on their younger sibling when they feel the baby is getting an undue amount of attention.

Donald

We were consulting with an office of five employees, with one of them a new hire, who also happened to be young in age. The two oldest employees (in chronological age) tended to mother this young, new employee. A third employee, who had been in the office for about a year and a half, and who had been the "baby" until that time, was now experienced enough not to need regular assistance. She began to feel ignored as the others mothered and constantly helped the new hire, and she began to show signs of resentment. She would continually go to the manager with petty complaints about how the new hire was doing some things. We advised the manager to give additional assistance and praise to this more experienced employee and to have her help train the new person. This added attention and trust turned her around, and she went on to help the new person learn the job quickly.

3. The attention given to a baby can cause other employees to project their resentment onto the newcomer directly. If you had a younger brother or sister (or if you were the baby in your own family), we're sure you experienced the following dynamic at some point. The youngest in the family has been getting a lot of attention, and the older children are tired of it. They look for an opportunity to do something and flaunt the fact that the youngest is either unable or not allowed to do it. It could be using a new toy, putting makeup on for the first time, or even something as simple as staying up late for a television show. The same thing can happen in an office if, after the first few weeks of general orientation, co-workers perceive the new "baby" of the office is becoming the manager's "pet." It is very important for managers to remember to pay attention to and provide praise for positive action by their experienced employees. Never take any employee for granted.

If you want a baby, have a new one. Don't baby the old one.

—Jessamyn West
To See the Dream

Tips from Managers

1. Get employees doing the most they can as soon as they can.

2. Protect new employees, but give them space to grow.

3. Let new employees make mistakes as long as they learn and don't repeat them.

4. Catch the "baby" doing something right and encourage it—you do it with your young children all the time!

5. Observe and manage the relationship that develops among existing office members and their new sibling—it can make your job easier or it can make it a nightmare.

6. Don't let age or seniority get in the way of putting the right person in the right job.

7. Don't let employees use their "baby" status as an excuse not to grow up. If you encounter this situation, keep the pressure on and they will either grow up or opt out.

8. Give the baby of the office the attention they need, but, as soon as possible, make extra attention unnecessary.

9. If you have a new employee who doesn't recognize their place in the organization (i.e., they are trying to assert themselves too much too soon), counsel them early on how to integrate into the office family rather than fight it.

10. When new employees come into your office, make sure you continue to give attention and praise to existing office family members.

Tips from Employees

1. When we're new, be clear with us what direction you want us to take.

2. Make it clear what your expectations are for our growth.

3. Share with the rest of the office family what you expect from us so nobody expects more (or less) than we are capable of delivering.

4. Let us have our space to grow when we want it.

5. Let us make mistakes without fear of losing our opportunity for career advancement.

6. Provide a "safety net" so we can make decisions without fear of failure.

7. Praise us when we do things right, but don't go overboard—we may be the baby of the office, but we're still adults.

8. Help us understand how to work with our office siblings, but remember we have to stand on our own two feet and develop our own working relationships.

9. If we can do the job, let us have the responsibility no matter what our seniority.

10. Don't forget the rest of us—we may not need as close guidance as the newcomer, but we still want (and need) attention.

CHAPTER 5

The Only Child: Too Much Management for Too Little Family

The only child has been called "the lonely one."

—Darrell Sifford
The Only Child

Doug

A few months after starting VALU Travel, after I'd had a chance to get a couple of markets going, we decided that we needed a salesperson who would focus on a couple of those markets while I continued to pursue and open other markets.

It was an interesting situation for me. Here I was, someone who regularly consulted with other businesses, attended many seminars, and read many books on business management. I was twenty-three years old, and I had an "Only Child."

At first, things worked well. We were both excited about the opportunities and the cutting-edge changes we were making. We enjoyed telling each other about our successes as well as talking about the "crazy" companies that didn't follow our advice. Things, however, got tougher as it went along.

I'm the type who enjoys change. I always like to think of the next mountain we can climb, or how we can climb this mountain faster. As a result, every time I got a great idea, my employee was the victim. In hindsight, that's really what he was—my victim. I realize now that many of the problems that occurred were my fault. I felt that I was a manager, so that's what I'd do—manage. As a result, I overmanaged.

Since that time I've learned that the key to managing a single employee is to be more in control and structured. Change is still good, in my opinion, but I have to be careful not to change the world in a day (or to try to change it every day).

Traditional thinking equates being an only child with loneliness and self-absorption. However, research shows that this is not necessarily true. Like all situations, there are pros and cons to being the only child or to having an only child. This is true in families *and* businesses. However, while more and more families are choosing to have just a single child due to later marriages, starting families at older ages, or the economics of raising children, businesses cannot grow if they remain one-employee enterprises. Therefore, it is usually just a new (or sometimes, fading) business that has just one employee. Or it might be a small department within a larger company.

Of course, unless the first birth in a family is twins or more, every family with children goes through a period of having an only child. With the explosive growth of small and home-based businesses in recent years, particularly with women owners, there has been an increase in the number of establishments starting out with one or two owners and one employee.

These businesses have some special needs that are very similar to the challenges and advantages of families with only children.

Characteristics of the Only Child

Only children are used to spending most of their time in an adult environment rather than with other children. Even when they have friends their own age, they spend a lot of time with their parents, where discussions and interests are on a more adult-centered level. The same is true in a single-employee work environment. There is a tendency for the single employee to become, at least socially, a part of the management environment, especially if there is just a single manager. This can be fine for the time being, but it can create great challenges when the business grows enough to require additional employees.

When single employees are brought too closely into the world of the manager, they can get frustrated and even resentful when it is necessary to do frontline tasks. This is especially true if managers tend to throw all the "dirty work" onto the employee and keep all the interesting, challenging tasks to themselves. The children and the parents, in these small businesses, work too closely together for the children not to realize that there is some interesting work that needs to be done, but that their parents don't give them the opportunity to do any of it.

On the other hand, if the manager goes overboard to share all the challenging activities, the parent and child become too much like co-managers without any employees. Such managers find themselves with no time to devote to the managerial activities of planning, organizing and building for the future. They can get mired in details that their employee is perfectly capable of handling. It is necessary to keep a balance. Each should cover the tasks appropriate for their positions, but management should provide the employee access to some varied, interesting work.

A single employee, like an only child, can find the experience somewhat lonely. It is part of the American culture for employees to get together and talk about their jobs and their lives. They frequently do not feel comfortable doing this with their manager, since part of what they talk about might be the normal complaining about their jobs and the conditions under which they work. Many people choose to work as much for the chance to be with other people during the day as for the income they earn. Such people do not generally do well in the "only child" scenario. People who are perfectly happy to do their own work without the typical chitchat of the office are better suited to such positions. Keep this in mind when you are hiring someone who will be an only employee. Seek a person who is self-contained and does not need the social atmosphere of a larger office.

If the person will be working in an office or department within a larger company, this problem is not as great. They will have peers with whom they can socialize during lunch or break times. This is more like the only child in a family that lives near relatives so the cousins can play together. The loneliness is more pronounced in the case of an independent office with a single employee that does not share a lunchroom or other gathering place with other employees.

In many offices and families, there is a great amount of responsibility placed on an only child. Just as a family with more than one child spreads the chores among the siblings, an office family with more than one subordinate distributes functions among all the office children. If one is having a bad day, others can fill in, knowing that the one they are helping today will help them out when they need it.

A single employee in an office lacks the same support from peers that an only child lacks by having no brothers or sisters. If the employee is not in a position to complete the assigned work, it must either be left undone, or the manager will have to take over. This can cause greater guilt, which often leads to resentment as the employee feels he or she is disappointing the manager. Managers in these situations can also get resentful if too often they have to complete work assigned to their subordinate.

With just one employee, managers find it considerably more difficult to be out of the office. This means less chance to take a vacation or even to take advantage of seminars or meetings that would help them learn ways to build the business or operate it more efficiently. It also means more pressure to come to work when sick. This is true of both the parent and the child. Each one feels a great responsibility to the other and does not want to let the other one down.

If single employees are given only the low-level work that managers don't want to handle, the result will be very dependent employees who are afraid to think for themselves or take any chances. However, if managers do allow employees to handle tasks that require initiative and creativity, the result will be more confident and capable employees. This is especially important in that emergency when the manager cannot be on the job and must depend on the employee. Many years ago, we became aware of what this can mean.

Doris

Karen was the only frontline employee in an office with two owners and a manager. She had been on the job for just a few months when her owners, a married couple, had to leave the country on business in the Orient. They were combining this business trip with a vacation since they were traveling so far. They left the office in the hands of their manager, who had been with them for many years, and Karen.

Two days after the owners had left town, the manager was in an automobile accident and was hospitalized. Although she recovered, she was seriously injured and could not be disturbed by Karen calling her from the office. The owners had by now finished their business meetings and were off on their own. Unfortunately, they had not left any information with Karen on where they could be reached.

Luckily, Karen was a very capable and intelligent person and had been allowed to do more than just clerical work in the office. In the short time she had been working there, she had been given a chance to learn at least a little about what was happening beyond her own position.

At first, of course, Karen was extremely frightened and frustrated. She then decided that she would go ahead and do the best she could to take care of things. She called on some of their customers and sales reps for help as needed and managed to get through the next ten days until the owners returned. The office did not fall apart, thanks to her feelings of self-confidence and her belief that the owners and manager would appreciate her efforts. She could just as easily have thrown up her hands and walked out when she came to work that day and found out that there was no "parent" on duty.

This example demonstrates the vulnerability of a single employee if the parents are suddenly and unexpectedly away and unreachable. When there are multiple employees, it is much easier to work as a team to try to meet the challenge. However, when there is just one, there is no one to share the responsibility if something happens. This is why it is very important that managers with just a single employee make sure that person is at least somewhat knowledgeable about the overall workings of the office. This is not a place for secrecy and "need to know" attitudes. If Karen had only been allowed to know just what she needed for her own job, she would never have been able to keep the office going when the owners and manager were both gone.

Another danger of having just one employee is not planning ahead for what will happen if that employee leaves. With more than one employee, it is possible to spread out the workload between management and the remaining staff and absorb the extra burden until a replacement can be hired. But with just one employee, all the work that person was doing will now fall on the manager, depriving the manager of the time to focus on management functions. The additional workload will make it even more difficult to replace the employee because of the time required for recruiting and interviewing candidates for the job.

This is one of the reasons why it is critical for new, small businesses to work hard to justify additional employees. An only-child office is not healthy in the long run. There is much more flexibility when there is more than one person to share the work and responsibilities. In this way, an office is different from a home family.

During any period when you do have just one employee, it is critical that you and the employee work hard to document whatever systems are in place. Have a working manual that explains step by step everything each person does. This way if someone leaves or gets sick, or you hire someone for any other reason, transition time will be minimized. For more on the importance of documenting work systems, we highly recommend *The*

E-Myth Revisited, by Michael Gerber. This book does such a good job of explaining why the worst thing that happens to many small businesses is that they grow beyond one or two employees (because they grow beyond the personal capabilities of the owner and now require real business systems), we won't even attempt to duplicate it here.

Parental Rivalry

Even though the single-employee office avoids the problems of sibling rivalry, there can be an opposite challenge when there are two or more owners or managers. The office with more managers than employees is top heavy and must work hard to avoid the problems this can create.

One of the challenges in a dual-management office with an only child is to avoid parental rivalry, where the co-managers vie with each other for the loyalty and friendship of the single employee. This is a very common problem and is extremely dangerous. The employee feels caught in the middle. In such situations, they will often try to play one parent against the other by offering to give or withhold loyalty from the parent being approached at the moment. Employees may also work so hard to avoid showing favoritism that they become totally frustrated. They may then resign and seek employment in a position without such pressures. This is the exact opposite to the more traditional problem of employee sibling rivalry.

Co-managers also have to avoid competing with each other for the employee's time. Since there is only one employee, there is a limit to how much work can be completed by this person. If each manager believes that his or her projects should take precedence, the employee will feel torn. The managers must decide together what the priorities of the office will be and then jointly request the employee to perform assignments they have agreed upon. They should not both be throwing projects at the employee without prior coordination.

Overparenting

Another challenge of an only-child office, just as with an only-child family, is the risk of "overparenting." Donald and Doug each like to joke that when they had only one child, it was easy to stay on top of the kid. When each of them had a second child, they and their wives were forced to go "man to man." Doris and Phil remember all too well that as soon as they had a third child, a "zone defense" was all they could manage.

While the inability to be as directly involved in everything a child does is somewhat frightening for parents who just added a second or third child to their family, it is usually a good thing for their children. It forces the children to handle things and grow up a bit more quickly on their own. It gives them more space for themselves. The same is true in an office with only one employee. It's easy for the employee to feel stifled by the constant attention and office parenting—and there's no sibling with which to share complaints. A second employee lifts some of this load and often makes for a better team environment.

Only-children offices with more than one manager also sometimes suffer from the "too many chiefs—not enough Indians" syndrome. In these offices, managers must accept the fact that they cannot confine themselves only to higher-level work, unless there is very little clerical type work that needs to be done. Each manager may have to take on a fair share of tasks that eventually will be assigned to subordinates when the business has grown enough to add support personnel.

As many parents have learned the hard way, it is easier to set family rules and regulations before there are lots of kids than to try to create new rules that the younger kids know their oldest sibling never had to live with. Similarly, the best time to develop policies and procedures in an office is when the business is new and small. When an office has one or two managers and only one employee, it might appear that you don't need written policies and procedures. However, all businesses should make their decisions with an eye to the future and make sure that their growth is accomplished smoothly rather than through major changes that disrupt and intimidate people.

With a very small staff, everyone knows everything that everyone else is doing. The manager has no trouble keeping up on everything that is happening in the office. As the business grows, however, this starts to change. It is important that procedures and systems are developed right from the beginning so that management will know what is happening without hearing every conversation and looking at every invoice and order form every day. It's always easier to deal with fires before they start.

Policies about compensation, vacation time, flexibility of hours, and other personnel matters should be developed for the future—not for the specific needs of the current employee. If policies are not developed carefully, trouble will develop later. The benefits and privileges that have been given to this sole employee will be taken for granted by that employee as time passes and will be expected to continue even when siblings come on the scene. Then, if new rules are made for the new employees because it's impossible to be as flexible as you were with just one employee, the original employee will expect to be exempted from any negative changes. This employee will also, however, expect to benefit from any "good" changes. If new employees are treated differently from the original one, there can be major resentment and sibling rivalry is virtually guaranteed.

The "Virtual" Only Child

There is an exception to this, however. This is for the "virtual" only child—someone who has been with the office a long time (usually longer than any other frontline person), is near retirement, and tends to work well alone on projects. The Dinkmeyers and McKay noted in *The Parent's Handbook* that children's places appear to be based on the chronological order of their birth. However, they go on to say that it isn't that simple. They describe a family with a thirteen-year-old son and two daughters, ages seven and five. The son doesn't play much with his sisters, preferring to be with his mom or by himself working with his models. Therefore, he sees himself more like an only child than an oldest child.

On the other hand, the older girl plays with her younger sister and enjoys teaching her to play games. She feels like a teacher to her younger sibling and views herself more like an oldest child.

This is very much like Phil's situation as he grew up.

Phil

When I was eight and my sister was sixteen, she went off to boarding school to finish high school. After high school, she came back home to live for a short time, until she got married at age nineteen and moved into a home with her husband. From the age of eight, with the exception of a little more than a year, I felt like an only child in terms of day-to-day life. Of course, the family was regularly in touch with my sister, but she and I did not share the daily sibling relationship that children living in the same home experience.

A similar relationship can exist within an office. When it does, it can create a unique form of sibling rivalry. But if handled properly, this can be limited. We had such an experience in our own office for a couple of years.

Doris

We had an employee, Marie, who had worked for us for more than twenty years, was over sixty-five years old, and was nearing retirement. Other than the manager, Phil, and me, the next closest employee to her in seniority had been with us for less than ten years and was considerably younger—very far from thinking about retirement. Marie was a very productive employee, but she had reached the stage where she liked to work primarily with her longtime clientele and particularly resisted taking new clients who were not planning major trips. She resisted doing straight airline tickets and other minor types of travel planning for new clients. She had also been allowed to reduce her work schedule from the normal, full-time, five-day work week to a three-day work week. She was, of course, only paid for the prorated shortened schedule.

Our newer, younger employees had not been offered the opportunity of a reduced schedule and were expected to take their fair share of any clients who came into or called the office, even if their potential purchase was not major. Periodically, we would get complaints from the younger staff that Marie was not willing to take new clients and that she wasn't sharing completely in the menial tasks that needed doing.

Marie was really in the position of a virtual only child, doing her own work, not overlapping with the siblings' work, and not relating to them much. We made it clear to the rest of the staff that, when they had more than twenty years with our company, were over sixty-five years old, and were as productive as Marie was with her longtime clients, we would be happy to do the same for them. This would stop the complaining for a few months as it helped them realize that Marie was in a different position, with a different history, and wasn't expected to take on the same "chores" as the rest of the staff.

Anytime you give a "favorite" status to an employee, you must be sure that you can defend the position that the employee being treated specially is not really a "true" and equal sibling—that there are real, meaningful reasons for the differences. Marie had little in common with the rest of the staff and was contributing as much or more to the profitability of the office as any of them. She had earned some special treatment by her many years of loyalty to the company.

When the New Baby Arrives

We discussed the baby of the family in the last chapter, but it is important to recognize here that only children in offices will almost always become older siblings at some time, unless they leave the company before a larger staff is needed. It is important to prepare "only employees" for plans to hire additional staff who will work side by side with them. Since a company only decides to increase staff when the current staff is suffering under the pressure of too much work with too few people, it would appear that the current employee would be thrilled at the addition of some help. However, there is frequently an underlying fear and potential resentment about what this new employee will do to the current structure and relationships within the office.

Once there are two employees, the division between managers and workers becomes more defined. The original employee is no longer in the same insider position with the manager as before and is more related in the pecking order to the new employee. They can feel rejected by management when they are no longer kept as close to the manager as before. They tend to try to hold on to their only-child status and make sure that they are still on the inside of knowing what is happening. They may try to lord it over the new employee that they know what is happening more than the new hire does.

Doug

After running the business for several years, we had ratcheted sales up so that I needed a sales assistant as well as an administrative assistant. I had an administrative assistant who was doing a good job and discussed the new position with her. We both decided that it wouldn't be a good position for her.

So we started searching for a new sales assistant. Simultaneously, I was seeking to hire some new outside salespeople. I came across a candidate who wasn't really right for the outside sales position but I thought could work really well in the sales assistant position. The only challenge was that he would need to take a slight pay cut and move halfway across the country. I told him about the opportunity and he accepted.

I was concerned that he wouldn't have the normal structure in place to deal with a new job opportunity, and part of my promise to get him to take the job was that I would mentor him as much as possible. So, when I was in town I'd take him out to lunch and talk more about sales situations, so he could learn how everything worked. Overall, things were working very well with him. The problem was that I never took the time to let my administrative assistant know why I was doing this and that she was important as well. The way she saw it, I was just taking the "new guy" to lunch and talking with him because I was taking her for granted or because I liked him more.

Unfortunately, I only found out about this at the exit interview. That's right, she quit, and I was back to hiring. I learned then that you need to let everyone know how important they are.

Asking the original employee to help teach the new hire how to do things can be a two-edged sword. How well it works will depend on the personality and self-confidence of the more experienced person. It may help the previously sole employee get to know the new person and even to become an older sibling protector. Or it may make them become a bullying, bossy surrogate parent. It is usually good to try this technique, but keep an eye on the situation, and step in, if necessary, if you find the bullying surrogate-parent role prevailing.

If the sibling rivalry gets too strong, you can set up a structure that helps the original employee become that "virtual" only child discussed earlier, working on his or her own without need to relate much to the new hire. However, in the long run, this is not a good idea, since it hampers the manager in being able to assign functions efficiently. It prevents a team spirit from developing and works well only when the virtual only child is near retirement.

If the former only child is expected to be around indefinitely, it is best to integrate the older sibling with the new baby and help them develop as a team. It will be easier when the third person is hired, just as it is usually easier at home with the third child than it is with the second child. How easy or hard the transition will be depends on how long the older one has been an only child in the office, the personalities of both people, and how differently the manager treats the original employee now that there is another frontline worker. As Dr. Benjamin Spock notes in *Baby and Childcare:* "Rivalrous feelings are often more intense in firstborn child[ren] because [they have] been used to the spotlight and [have] had no competition. A later child has already learned to share his parents' attention since birth."

Another challenge in bringing a second employee on board is managing the expectations of both the manager and the original employee. There is a tendency, especially where the relationship between the managers and the sole employee has been good, to expect the new hire to be like the original one and to work in the same manner. However, just as each child in the family is different from the others, you can expect the new hire to be quite different from the original one. The manager needs to help the former sole employee learn to accept someone doing things differently and reacting differently and not to judge the new person by the way they would have done the work. It is also sometimes difficult to get original employees to give up some functions to the new person, even when they have been complaining loudly about how overworked they are.

In her book, *Your Second Child—A Guide for Parents,* Joan Solomon Weiss quotes Dr. Brian Suttor Smith of the University of Pennsylvania about how a home with siblings can be a richer experience for both the children and their parents. Their family get-togethers are more festive and the emotional range is much greater in a family with more than one child. According to him, the lows may be lower, but the highs are higher and there are more times of "uproarious happiness." As he states, "Sure, kids can fight like the devil, but they can also have great times together."

"More than half of only children wish for siblings for companionship," Weiss continues. "Sisters and brothers won't necessarily like each other, but they will have a powerful and lasting impact on each other." Without siblings, there are no peers to join with you against management when things aren't the way you want. Being an only child can be more lonely in terms of peer relationships, but some people thrive on the chance to be by themselves and do not do well in the normal give and take of a bunch of siblings.

The growth of new small businesses is showing no signs of abating— in fact, these business are opening at record rates. Therefore, there will be an abundance of businesses for the foreseeable future that are home to only-child employees. Some will never grow beyond that level, but most will go on to add on employees as their businesses succeed and grow.

> At its best, being an only child can enhance the ability to work independently, to use your own initiative, to draw your own conclusions and solve your own problems.   —Darrell Sifford
> *The Only Child*

Tips from Managers

1. Don't fall into the habit of treating your sole employee as a co-manager.

2. Don't just heap the dirty work onto your subordinate. Make sure to provide some challenging, interesting tasks as well.

3. Encourage your employee to take vacation time, and do the same yourself. Everyone needs a chance to recharge.

4. Make sure your employee has reasonably good knowledge of the overall workings of the office, so that, in an emergency, if you are not available, he or she will be able to carry on for at least a short time.

5. Have a contingency plan for what you will do if your only employee resigns. Don't wait until it happens to decide what actions you need to follow.

6. If you are a co-manager, avoid competing with the other manager for the loyalty and friendship of the employee. Even if your co-manager falls into that trap, don't allow yourself to be brought into it.

7. Be aware of the potential for that "virtual" only child if you have a long-term employee, near retirement, who just doesn't fit in with a newer, younger staff.

8. Make sure you are making decisions that will work when you have more than one subordinate.

9. Have a written policy and procedures manual that can carry you into the time when the business has grown. It's easier to do this from the beginning than to create it after you've gotten employees used to things that won't work with a larger staff.

10. Work to build the business so you won't always be dependent on just one employee. A family can be effective in the long term with just one child, but a business needs more if it is truly to succeed.

Tips from Employees

1. Be friendly with me, but don't consider me your "best friend." I have other friends outside the office.

2. Even if you are willing to work late every night and want to keep your expenses under control, it isn't fair to expect me to work overtime regularly.

3. Even though we are a small office, I still need to have opportunities for development.

4. Don't put too much pressure on me since I am the only one here. I can still only do just so much in a day, and I will break under too much pressure.

5. Sometimes, I feel lonely without any co-workers. It would be nice if you could occasionally send me to a meeting or seminar where I can mingle with peers.

6. Please don't "dump" all the dirty work on me and do all the interesting work yourself. I am a valued employee, not a servant.

7. Please keep me informed about what is happening so that I can feel a part of the overall business.

8. Understand that the business has to grow to succeed and that, at some time, you will have to bring in more staff even though the additional expense will be a risk. Otherwise, I am likely to get burned out and leave.

9. Let me know when you are considering hiring an additional employee. It would even be a good idea to let me meet the prospects you are considering and give you my opinion.

10. Let me help you train a new employee. It will help make me feel a part of the growth rather than threatened by it.

CHAPTER 6

Pick-ers and Pick-ees:
Why Do They Always Pick on Me?

Isn't it interesting how we can be perfectly nice to a stranger and then rude to those closest to us?

—Loni Anderson as Jennifer on *WKRP in Cincinnati* describing, in her words, their "office family"

Murray and Ted. Carla and Cliff. Bill and Matthew.

What do they have in common? If you're like us and watch too much television, then you know that Murray, Carla, and Bill are constant pick-ers— i.e., people who were always picking on another co-worker. Ted, Cliff, and Matthew were always the pick-ees—the people picked upon. The shows were, respectively, *The Mary Tyler Moore Show, Cheers,* and *NewsRadio.*

We've all seen pick-ers and pick-ees in our office environment—those people who constantly try to raise themselves up by putting others down and those who always seem to be the butt of all jokes at the water cooler. While this makes for great storytelling in sitcoms and movies, the reality is that it doesn't make for cohesive, productive teamwork.

So what do parenting experts tell us about kids and teamwork, and what does it mean to us when we're "parenting the office"? In *How Good Parents Raise Great Kids,* Alan and Robert Davidson discuss some of the critical elements that parents must teach their children to nurture their socialization skills. We find that these skills are just as important for managers to teach and develop with their subordinates as they are for parents to teach their children. According to the Davidsons, socially successful people:

1. Fit into society comfortably. They make a contribution and easily become part of a team.

2. Make a good impression on strangers. They are more likely to start off on the good side of people. They are interesting, so people tend to want to get to know them.

3. Communicate through good listening and talking skills. They are both able to express themselves among others and able to listen and understand where other people are coming from. They effectively get their ideas across.

If this sounds like exactly the kind of skills and characteristics we want in people who are in our office, don't be surprised—it's another example of "parenting the office." We've frequently given advice to owners and managers to recruit and promote people with these sorts of skills. There's a tendency to hire and promote on the basis of technical skill alone, i.e., by asking the question, "Who is the best at their current job?"

However, we've found that more important questions are, "Who can effectively work with their peers, supervisors, and subordinates? Who has the abilities to improve their position within the company and earn people's respect?" These people will form the nucleus of a solid team, rather than becoming "pickers" or constantly being followed by a "black cloud" and becoming "pick-ees."

So what does it take for someone to become successful on a team? The Davidsons' list includes:

• Negotiation skills
• Cooperation skills
• A sense of identity
• The ability to deal with peer pressure
• The ability to make friends

Negotiation Skills

Life is full of negotiations. It's not a long leap from children deciding what to play to manager and worker agreeing on the schedule for completion of a project. We find three of the negotiating lessons the Davidsons teach to be as useful in parenting an office as in parenting a home. At first glance, some of them may seem a bit simple. Why, you may ask, would I need to work with adults in the office in the same mode I would with my children at home? In our experience in our own office and consulting with many other companies, it is clear to us that just because we hire adults does not mean we can assume they understand negotiations. In fact, it's quite the contrary. The result is that there are few lessons that are "too childish" to communicate.

1. Teach negotiation by demonstrating it. *Quid pro quo,* the art of giving something in exchange for something in return (in Latin, it literally translates as "something for something"), is as old as human interaction itself. It's the most basic form of negotiation, and it's a necessary component of socialization and teamwork. The wheels of society turn on giving and getting, and parents of both home and office should model good negotiation skills as part of developing their children and staff.

At home, this may be as simple as teaching kids the absolute basics. The Davidsons suggest demonstrating with children by striking simple bargains with them. Offer a special treat if chores are done on time, for example. This is distinctly different from the bribery of offering a child candy to get them to stop crying. The latter demonstrates and reinforces extortion by proving a positive reaction can result from a negative action; the former is a normal negotiation that proactively offers a tangible reward in exchange for the child's good behavior.

Parents can also let their children see them negotiating with others. Let them hear you deal with a repairman, the car salesman, etc. In our family, Doris and Phil were always very open with the kids about money and negotiations. It would often be the subject of dinner conversations either directly or indirectly. The result was that all three kids grew up with a healthy understanding of how these things worked and were rarely fooled by various manipulative sales or marketing tactics. By contrast, one of the children married someone from a family where money and "adult" negotiations were constantly hidden from the children because it wasn't "appropriate" for open discussion. The lack of early education meant those kids had to learn things the hard way when they became adults.

If this kind of openness is required to teach the simple aspects of negotiation to children at home, imagine how much it helps in offices where negotiations are complex and much more is at stake! Yet we often find that managers are more like the parents above who never discuss these things in the open. Certainly, corporate interests often require that not everything be talked about publicly. However, it is rare that a manager doesn't have many opportunities to directly negotiate with their subordinates at work and also to give them insight into how the company negotiates with its customers and how managers negotiate with vendors, other managers, bosses, etc. If these negotiations are totally hidden, as is often the case, how then are employees supposed to know what to do when the boss isn't around? More importantly, how are they supposed to grow and be prepared for a day when they are now the leader who must negotiate?

This is often referred to as the "mushroom theory of management"— keep employees in the dark and feed them manure, and expect them to grow. It just doesn't happen. When these employees grow into management positions, they have to learn things the hard way just as Phil and Doris's in-law had to learn. It's much better to share in the open whenever possible and allow employees to grow in a monitored environment.

2. Encourage your children to make their own decisions. The only way for children to learn how to make good decisions is to practice making them. When parents constantly make decisions for their children, they harm them in two ways. First, they deny them the opportunity to grow through the process, often resulting in children who grow up dependent on others to make decisions for them. Perhaps more importantly, yet more subtly, they send the message to their children that the children aren't capable of making good decisions on their own. This leads to an even more insidious form of dependency later in life.

The same is true at work. Office parents must let their subordinates make their own decisions. It, too, is the only way for them to grow. Making decisions for employees may feed the manager's ego, but it promotes a dependent, often ineffective workforce. In today's fast-paced, "lean and mean" corporate culture, businesses can't afford to require employees to wait for managers to make every decision. The window of opportunity may be lost to a competitor, or the moment of truth to impress the customer goes down the drain.

Jan Carlzon, former president of the Scandinavian Airline System, made a wonderful analogy in his book, *Moments of Truth,* an excellent examination of how he changed the corporate culture at the airline from a product-focused business to a customer-centered one. He compared managing an office to coaching a football (soccer to us Americans) team. Imagine, he said, a forward dribbling the ball towards the goal all alone, only to have to stop just inside the eighteen-yard line to run to the sideline and ask the coach whether and where he should shoot. The opportunity would be lost, and any self-respecting player would be uninterested in playing for a coach who didn't trust them to make these decisions for themselves.

Sports is often an excellent microcosm of good parenting skills in both home and office. Parenting experts routinely advise mothers and fathers how to prepare their children for the realities of the world and how to teach them to not only be productive in their own right but also effective members of a team. Few youngsters ever grow up to be professional athletes, so we've found that the sports field serves even better for teaching teamwork than preparing anyone for a livelihood on the playing field.

We experienced a moment of serendipity as we were writing this chapter. Just as we were thinking of the difference in parenting styles between those who reserve all decisions for themselves versus those who understand that children and employees alike need opportunities to decide for themselves to be successful, we heard a story on National Public Radio about how the National Basketball Association Finals that year reflected a different, more open, and trusting management style. Gone from the NBA Finals were the yellers and screamers who didn't coach but rather tried to control every player's movements all the time. In their place were two of the NBA's finest modern coaches, Phil Jackson and Larry Bird.

They coached their teams, the Los Angeles Lakers and Indiana Pacers respectively, by preparing them before the game and trying to make sure that they had the right people in the right place at the right time. During the game, you rarely saw them say a word. They let their players make their own decisions and trusted that all the preparation they did beforehand would suffice. They realized that in the heat of the game, they had to allow their players to make their own decisions.

3. Let your children learn the consequences of poor decisions. If parents let their children practice making decisions, then they have to be prepared to let them make bad ones. The only way to learn to avoid the bad ones is to suffer through the consequences of some. It's the only way children will ever learn to take responsibility for the natural and logical consequences of their actions—a very important concept that we explore in more detail in a later chapter.

Doris and Phil

A friend of ours, Joe, told us of one of those moments where children finally have the epiphany that there are consequences to their decisions and that not everything in life is an entitlement. Joe's sixteen-year-old son was living with his mother. One day, his son called Joe "just to chat." Sensing that this was a bit of a setup, Joe asked his son if he needed something. Sure enough, he asked his father if he could have $200. Joe asked him what he wanted the money for. He replied that he wanted to get a new baseball glove and spikes so he could try out for the school baseball team.

Joe asked him if he thought that was wise, and he seemed a bit put off by the question. He knew that his grades hadn't been anywhere near where his capability was, so he wasn't quite sure how to answer the question. Joe suggested that he take the time he wanted to spend on baseball and put it into schoolwork, since the benefits of his education would last long beyond the baseball season. Joe told him he would be happy to give him the money—next year, if he got his grades up.

Naturally, he was disappointed. He got over his anger, however, and came to the realization that he had dug his own hole. Joe had often told him of the importance of focusing on school and getting a summer job, but he had always been too laid-back and lazy to pursue either with any gusto. It had hurt that he wasn't taking his father's advice, but Joe knew that all of his "speechifying" would never have much of a direct impact. Joe had to let him make his own decisions and live with the consequences. Now he realized that without a job, he didn't have his own money; and without the good grades he and Joe knew he could get, he wasn't going to be entitled to his father's support for something that was not essential.

After this incident, Joe could tell that their relationship (and his son) matured. Joe was no longer just a human ATM, and his son began to feel more accountable for his own decisions.

It's no different with the people who work for us in an office. Sometimes we know that an employee is making a bad decision, but arguing or correcting them will have no effect. We have to give them their rope and, if necessary, allow them to hang themselves. Actually, we don't want them to hang themselves—just choke a little so they remember not to do it again!

Seriously, we obviously won't allow employees to make decisions that would harm them, their co-workers, customers, or company, but we do have to give them some room to learn on their own. Phil remembers an experience he had as an executive many years ago.

Phil

I was running the education and training department of a major trade association in Washington, D.C. I had hired a very capable and aggressive, but somewhat inexperienced, employee to put together a series of workshops around the country. She had run individual dinner seminars before, but this was her first time with something of this magnitude.

As she was putting this program together, I could tell she wasn't "dotting the i's and crossing the t's" as I knew from my experience she needed to do. With programs of this size, the devil really is in the details. But she was young, a bit naïve, and headstrong.

I could have sat down with her and directed her step by step on what to do. But I could tell that she didn't think these steps were necessary. I would just be coming across like her father, laying down the law (the twenty-year difference in our ages and experience would have only emphasized this perception as well). Even if the program went off flawlessly if I interfered, she would never have attributed the success to the forced attention to details. We'd have a successful series, but what would she or we learn from it?

We had chosen accomplished speakers and had an experienced on-site staff, so I knew nothing could go too wrong. I warned her that I thought she wasn't planning to the level of detail my experience told me she should, but I also emphasized it was her show to run however she wanted.

Sure enough, a number of things went wrong. One hotel meeting room had the wrong AV equipment, and the speaker at another showed up late due to a miscommunication. We even lost $1,000 at one meeting because she forgot to call in to reduce the guaranteed number of meals.

When we did our "postmortem" of the series, she was painfully aware of the shortcomings. The education we delivered was fine, and no one was hurt, but there was a lot more stress and on-site work than there should have been. She volunteered that she hadn't planned the details enough; she was surprised at how much more work a series of events was than just the sum of the individual events she had done so well before.

We all want our "children" not to have to learn things the hard way— if only they'd listen to us! Just like my kids growing up, though, I knew this was a lesson she wouldn't take from me unless she went through the pain of her own mistakes. Now, she wasn't going to make this mistake again, and except for a little embarrassment, no one was hurt. We did have that loss of $1,000, but that was a small price to pay for the lesson she learned!

Cooperation Skills

Most businesses are only as good as the group effort of the employees. No matter how good the individual, success is based as much on interaction with the team as it is on pure personal talent. Synergy, that often-spoken yet rarely enacted buzzword of business, occurs when the whole is greater than the sum of its parts. Simply put, that takes teamwork. Parenting experts' advice on teaching teamwork to children also works for managers teaching their employees.

*"Let me be the first to say we're
very impressed with the way
you've united the office, Sally."*

"Let your child help plan activities," advise parenting experts. Let them
help plan their birthday party and the family vacation. Through this, they
not only feel a greater sense of ownership, but they also come to understand the "give and take" needed to reach an agreement. All members of
a family have their own tastes, so let them decide what is most important
to them and what they must be willing to give up.

While adults in the office may (and we emphasize *may*) have the maturity to intuitively understand that there is always a "give and take" in
office activities, assignments, etc., this doesn't eliminate the benefits of
allowing them to help plan activities. This doesn't mean that managers
should abdicate their responsibility to make the tough decisions, leaving
everything to "the team" to decide. It does mean that it is usually a good
idea to involve people in the process. The benefits are numerous.
Everyone feels more of a sense of ownership in these plans and thus will
more likely tolerate the things they wish were different. They, and the
manager, get a better understanding of what's important to each individual, and they continue to grow and build their negotiation skills, which
can only help with customers and future promotions.

These same parenting experts also tell us to encourage our kids to
engage in volunteer activities. These activities expose children to situations where they need to cooperate and communicate.

Doris and Phil

One of the defining moments of Doug's teen years was when he became involved in a fraternal youth organization. This was his first real chance to be part of something on his own without any significant family involvement. Doug quickly found his own identity in this group and rose to lead it.

He got along great with some members and the adults who watched over the group but didn't get along well with others. Before, he would just have been argumentative with anyone with whom he disagreed. As the leader, however, he realized that he needed to find ways to get everyone to participate in his vision. He learned how to get along better with others and motivate even people he didn't particularly like, in a way that he never could have learned in our home. Not only was his growth tremendous, but he was able to put these lessons to use in college as Student Government president and later as the youngest regional sales manager at Hertz and VP of Business Development in our own company.

We encountered a similar situation with a small business with whom we were consulting. They had a manager who was two years away from retiring. The owner had already decided she wanted Debbie, another employee, to take over. Her problem was that Debbie had never had any managerial experience. She had just named Debbie the "assistant manager" so it was clear she was the "heir apparent," but the office wasn't large enough for her to get much experience, particularly since the existing manager was such a large presence.

We suggested that Debbie be encouraged to volunteer for a leadership position with a local organization and get experience there. It turned out Debbie was active in her church and had always thought about doing more but had never had the motivation to step up. She volunteered first to run the church's Spring Carnival and then became a vice-president the next year. Needless to say, this experience prepared her well to take over the office!

Office parents should encourage employees to be active in community organizations. The cooperation skills they will gain from such activities will help them on the job.

A Sense of Identity

To be prepared to cope with the many challenges and temptations life throws them, children need to develop a healthy sense of identity. Parenting experts talk of the importance of a child's identity and how it affects and is affected by their self-esteem. While self-esteem and a clear sense of identity are based on a myriad of things, there are a couple of tactics recommended for parents at home that can also be used to parent the office.

1. Expose them to literature and magazines. Learning and growing never stop. Whether parenting the home or the office, exposing people to reading opens up new ideas and helps them understand who they are and how they fit in. Doug has used reading successfully as a core principle in his life and business management style.

Doug

I've always believed that reading is an integral part of professional growth. For many years, I've made sure to read at least six relevant books a year plus a variety of trade and general-interest magazines.

I took the same approach in both managing teams and consulting with customers. Every employee I had in my sales organization was put on a customized reading program. I would regularly clip articles from the press and route them around, asking my employees to think about what this meant for them.

This also worked well with consulting clients. I've found that many people don't take the time to just get away from the daily grind and read. We identified a list of five or six books that would be real eye openers for our clients and we suggested they read them. We even ended up buying them wholesale to resell, so that when we recommended a book we could just get it to them without having to rely on them to go to the bookstore on their own. It was that important!

2. Add on to their responsibilities and then praise their success. *Parenting for Dummies* says, "When they say they can't, let them know they can do anything—if they just try."

Donald

I had a new employee once who was hired to test some sophisticated mathematical software. The designers and programmers were very experienced, and she was more than a little nervous about her new job.

She had excellent mathematical training and clearly had the common sense that is needed to test things well. However, when faced with new challenges, she also had a penchant for questioning whether she could really rise to the occasion. She was by far the most junior member of the team and really doubted her abilities compared to the rest of us.

During her first few weeks on the job, she would express her uncertainties to me once or twice a week. Each time, I would reinforce in her my belief that she could do the job, and I would work with her to break her tasks down to the next one or two baby steps.

I ended up having to take a trip that kept me largely out of touch for a full week. When I came back, she asked to meet with me. She told me she really didn't feel as though she had been contributing. Almost breaking down, she essentially offered to quit. I had a nice discussion with her about what she had accomplished to date, and what she needed to do to continue to build her confidence.

Later that day, she was with me and my technical lead discussing a rather complicated part of the model. She quickly contradicted him when he said something wrong, and on several occasions she led the discussion and taught me things about what we were doing.

When the meeting was over, I asked her to stay for a moment. I closed the door and literally said, "What was this morning's talk all about?" She was uncertain how to respond until I continued, "You were so worried about whether you could really handle this job. You just spent an hour teaching me things and correcting others when they said something wrong. I really don't think you have to worry."

It's been a long while since she's come to me afraid again!

Parenting for Dummies adds, "Independence and self-confidence begin when you let your children do things for themselves that you normally do for them." The first time we let an employee do something themselves, they are filled with the same pride and self-esteem children feel the first time they put on their own clothes, operate the VCR, or do other things that would seem mundane to us yet are so exciting to them.

The Ability to Deal with Peer Pressure

Every child encounters peer pressure, but it doesn't stop just because they grow up. Though perhaps a bit more subtly than children, adults in the office still exert and are influenced by peer pressure. There are often unwritten rules (or office norms) about not shining too brightly, not reaching too far. In the worst of cases, peer pressures cause employees to engage in dishonest, unethical, even illegal activities, much as peer pressure can drive teenagers to use drugs or commit acts of theft or vandalism—acts they would never do on their own.

What parenting techniques work to help parents deal with peer pressure? We've found that the two best ways to counterbalance peer pressure with our kids is to (1) expose them to many different controlled environments and (2) consistently engage them ourselves in conversation and joint activities. Exposure to controlled environments—for example, preschools and summer camps—gives children a chance to see many different views but never get so close to any one that they lose sight of the others. Engaging your children yourself on a regular basis is equally important. We may not be able to control their thoughts and actions, but we can certainly be an influence—only if we invest the time to stay involved. A third, but important, technique is to serve as a role model. Make sure you are not making decisions based on what others do. Be willing to stand tall yourself.

What does this have to do with an office environment? An awful lot! A good friend of ours refers to a major part of his job as a manager as being "Adult Day Care." In many ways, he's not joking. The same two elements—exposing employees to different controlled environments and consistently engaging them ourselves—are keys to successful office parenting.

The Ability to Make Friends

A key to every child and adult's ability to function in a team is the ability to make friends. When we examine those "pick-ees" we mentioned at the start of this chapter, we find that one of their fundamental weaknesses is that they don't make friends very well. In fact, they tend either to keep very shallow friendships (e.g., Cliff's "friendship" with Norm on *Cheers*) or to chase away what few people there are who try to befriend them (e.g., the character of Ted Baxter and his attitude towards normally friend-to-everyone Mary Richards in *The Mary Tyler Moore Show*). Some people make and lose friends with such regularity that they probably don't stop often to think about what it takes to make friends. We find there are three critical factors.

1. Openness and a willingness to share. Children and adults alike make friends more easily when they are open and show a willingness to share. Little kids share toys, while adults share ideas, but the behavior is essentially the same.

2. Interest in other people. Friendship often means doing things for other people without the direct expectation of anything in return. This takes a genuine interest in other people.

3. Ability to interact. True friendship involves a special kind of camaraderie. Some of our fondest memories of childhood friends and the

moments we shared involve friendly teasing. Making friends often involves the ability to interact and judge that fine line between fun teasing and going too far. "Pickers" tend to go too far, and "pick-ees" tend to be easy targets. In mutually fun teasing, we usually target someone who can take it and even give it back a bit. Donald describes a couple of situations where teasing was all part of the game of teamwork.

Donald

My unit in the air force was notorious for going-away celebrations that turned into the most uproarious roasts. By the end of the presentations, we were all in stitches. Somehow, we found a way to walk that fine line and never truly offend anyone, but we sure came close. Of course, in this type of situation, you have to be prepared to get as much as you give!

When I left the air force and began working in a small business and then running one with the family, this was one of the elements I truly missed. When I moved to a midsize software-consulting company, one of the things I immediately fell in love with was our "Fab Fridays." The last Friday of each month, the company treats everyone to lunch. We celebrate anniversaries, good things happening to the company, and birthdays. There are always a few moments of good, clean, team fun. The emcee would always say a few amusing things, and the audience was free to heckle.

New employees do not introduce themselves; they introduce each other. They pair off and have about forty seconds to learn about their partner. All the while, the audience is singing out the tune to Jeopardy. *Birthday people compete in contests for a gift certificate. One month it was a watermelon-eating contest (no hands, of course); another it was a hula-hoop contest in keeping with the Hawaiian theme for that meal. All of it is pretty corny, but it is a chance to interact with each other outside the often serious lines of daily work.*

It's nice having all the children together again.
—McLean Stevenson as Henry Blake on *M*A*S*H*
in a scene where Trapper, Hawkeye, Frank, and
Margaret are bickering after Trapper and Hawkeye
tricked Margaret into rescinding her request for a transfer

Tips from Managers

1. Hire and promote people for their people skills, not just technical skills.

2. Demonstrate negotiation skills to employees by engaging in simple negotiations with them.

3. Allow subordinates to see and hear you negotiate with others in the company and with customers.

4. Encourage employees to make as many decisions as possible themselves.

5. Let your people deal with the consequences of poor decisions—it won't be the end of the world.

6. Share planning activities with those who work for you.

7. Encourage your "office kids" to be volunteers within the company and with local organizations.

8. Expose your employees to books, magazines, and other useful reading materials.

9. Give your subordinates added responsibility as quickly as you can, and praise them when they can handle it. Let them do as much by themselves as they can (and even a little they can't).

10. Engage your staff one on one personally to ensure they don't fall victim to peer pressure.

Tips from Employees

1. Help us build and practice our people skills as much as you tend to focus on working on our technical skills.

2. Share the negotiations you have within the company and with customers to teach us how and why you negotiate the way you do.

3. Let us make as many decisions as we can ourselves.

4. We know we should be accountable for our own poor decisions, but make us feel comfortable that we really can risk this.

5. Involve us in planning activities.

6. When we seek opportunities to be more involved, reward us for our initiative.

7. Let us know where it would be valuable for us to volunteer within our company and with local organizations to practice leadership skills.

8. Share with us ideas of what we should read—if you got something from it, we might as well.

9. Give us responsibility. Sometimes it may cause you extra work, but in the long run, our growth will be worth it.

10. Tell us what we need to do to advance our careers. If we're a pick-ee, help us do what we need to do to change people's impression of us.

CHAPTER 7

He Says, She Says:
Disorder in Families and the Office

United we stand—divided we fall. —George Pope Morris

Doris

I had recently promoted one of our employees, Carol, to assistant manager. One of her primary functions was supervising employee leave. Employees needed to get Carol's approval for any voluntary leave and she was responsible for making sure the office was adequately staffed.

Carol tended to be somewhat strict about allowing time off, since she didn't want to take any chances that we would be shorthanded. I, on the other hand, tended to be rather liberal in granting leave, figuring that, if we were a little understaffed, we'd manage to get through the day, and our employees would feel good that we tried our best to be flexible with them.

Needless to say, one Monday when Carol was out, a junior employee came to me to ask if she could take off Thursday of the following week. She knew Carol would be back in the office on Tuesday and that the request could have waited; but she also knew that, since one person was already scheduled for leave on that Thursday, she had a much better chance of getting her wish from me than from Carol.

Without looking at the leave schedule, I carelessly told her that she could have the day, forgetting that this was no longer my responsibility. When Carol came back the next day and found out about my granting time off to an employee, she was, rightfully, quite annoyed. She pointed out to me that there was already someone else scheduled to be out and that the request was not an emergency and could have waited.

I had to admit to her that I had overstepped my bounds since I had del-egated this responsibility to her. I apologized to Carol and made it quite clear to the staff that from that time on, unless it was a dire emergency, they were not to request leave from me or Phil, even if we were the "top bosses." We, of course, had to honor my granting of the time off in this case since it had already been done.

Several times over the next few months, one or another employee tried to come to me for permission for leave; but, keeping my promise to Carol, I merely reminded them that I was no longer in charge of that decision. They soon learned that it was worthless to ask me, and the attempt to play one of us against the other in this particular area stopped.

Have you ever watched a child play one parent against the other? Did you or your siblings do this with your parents? Do your children play this game with you and your spouse?

Susie knows that Dad believes in independence while Mom is some-what protective. So, Susie, being a reasonably smart eight-year-old, waits until Mom is out to ask Dad if she can go to her new friend Jane's house. Mom's response would probably be, "No, not until I meet your friend and talk to her parents." But she knows Dad will say yes without ever bother-ing to meet Jane or speak with her parents. The worst that can happen is that Dad will surprise her and say no, but Susie is sure that Mom will for-bid it until she has more information.

In any office where there is more than one manager, it is critical to set up guidelines and policies that let everyone know just who is responsible for what in order to avoid these types of games from the staff. This is true whether there are two or more equal managers (typical in a small business with two or three partners), if the office has a manager/assistant manager hierarchy, or if the office is part of a larger organization so there are multi-ple managers in a hierarchy. All managers and all subordinates must know who is in charge and when. This, of course, takes coordination and planning on the part of the management team to establish clear policies and imple-ment them consistently (the mistake Doris made once but never again!). In addition, these roles must continually be reviewed and revised as necessary. Nothing is written in stone—if situations change, the roles can change.

In the hustle and bustle of daily life, parents often find it difficult to coor-dinate policies at home, and it's no different for office parents. To achieve a reasonable level of coordination, managers should meet regularly, away from the staff, to discuss what has been happening in the office and to set any new policies that may now be needed. The management team should

"Perkins, I'm beginning to have my doubts that
the other manager lets you do it this way."

also revise any old policies that have been causing confusion or challenges. These meetings can be held in the office after hours, when the rest of the staff is gone for the day, or at the home of one of the managers. If it is impossible to get together after hours, then co-managers should leave the office for lunch together to discuss office matters away from the employees. Sometimes, especially for reorganizations or other such major changes, it is even a good idea for the co-managers to get away together in a relatively relaxed atmosphere for a full day or two to discuss the changes and make plans without distractions. This is really no different from parents who take a few moments after the kids are in bed to discuss issues or otherwise find time away from their children to sort out important challenges they face.

One way or another, it is critical for managers to communicate with each other to cover any questions or problems that have arisen and that might cause difficulties in the future. This can range from formal meetings, to email or phone calls, to chatting when they conveniently bump into each other. The key is to avoid the trap of no communication, leaving the field ripe for subordinates to play one manager against another. Many crises can be avoided if some care is taken in the early stages.

Where Co-Managers Are Real Spouses

One special scenario is when the office co-parents are actually spouses and co-parents in their home. Such a team must be careful not to automatically bring the same role definitions to the office as they have in their home. Even when office and home parents are the same people, the roles and strengths might be quite different in both places.

Doris and Phil

We have consulted with several small businesses with a common problem—a husband who, on retiring from a career in an executive position, decides to join his wife in her small business. In most cases, the wife has been making a small to moderate profit and that has satisfied her. Her husband, however, has now joined the company and is going to use his skills to grow the business and increase the profit.

One case in particular demonstrates what can happen if the couple is not careful, although the details of the arrangement obviously differ from case to case. In this case, the wife, Ruth, was an excellent salesperson and had built the volume of her business very well. However, she was not making a profit when she first came to us for help. We helped her realize that there were some sales she didn't really want and that she was confusing volume of sales with profitability. She won accounts primarily by undercutting any competitor's bid, thereby losing money at times. It had taken us a couple of years to help Ruth turn her business around, until her volume was about half what it was but she was now making a reasonable profit on those sales.

Her husband, Jack, retired and decided to join her in the business to help build sales. He wasn't interested in any outside help since he had been an executive and believed that he could teach his wife how to make this a "real" business.

In their private lives, Jack was, without question, the dominant partner, with Ruth usually accepting his decisions with few questions. When he joined her in the business, this relationship came over with him. Although Ruth understood the peculiarities of this small business much better than Jack did, he became the decision maker for the business just as he was at home.

Jack purchased a very expensive automated system that would handle the great growth in sales that he was going to create. He made other financial commitments before the sales became real. This great growth in sales never materialized and, eventually, the couple went bankrupt.

If he had joined the business and worked with his wife, using the same pattern that had worked for the past couple of years, they would have enjoyed a comfortable income and working together in a successful business.

But his grandiose ideas without knowledge of the business, and her insecurity and unwillingness to challenge him, doomed the company to failure.

Define Each Manager's Role

What is important when spouses work together is that their roles be defined and made known to all involved. The roles should be assigned based on each partner's strengths and weaknesses, not on their roles at home. The best way to do this is to state the basic areas of responsibility in a written office policy manual and to remind all staff members of any areas that are presenting challenges.

In *Parenting for Dummies,* Sandra Hardin Gookin and Dan Gookin describe the following simple rules for maintaining consistency in parenting:

1. Think before you say something.

2. Make your rules realistic.

These are equally applicable to office situations, whether the managers are married to each other or not. Rule number one would have helped Doris avoid approving a request that was not hers to approve. Before answering a subordinate's request, ask yourself if you already have a policy covering the request. If not, is this likely to be a request that might come from someone else at another time? If the answer to this question is yes, consider getting together with your co-manager and create a policy to cover it before giving a hasty answer.

Rule number two will help you avoid making rules that you can't enforce.

Phil

In our early years running our travel agency, we decided that all client reservation records should be kept in a central location so that, if an agent was out of the office, the information would still be easily available to everyone. When the office was small and computers weren't yet on the scene, the system worked fairly well.

However, as the staff grew, this system became cumbersome. Agents had to leave their desks regularly to retrieve the file for a client whose trip was in a highly active planning stage. By now, computers had also come into the office scene and all records that involved flight arrangements were stored in the computer. Records of clients taking just a cruise or tour with no air arrangements were not in the computer at that time; they were only on the written reservation records.

The staff began to complain to Doris about having to constantly go and retrieve records. The new assistant manager agreed with the staff that it would be much easier and more efficient if the agents were able to keep active records on their own desks.

However, Doris believed that without the centralization of the records, it would be very difficult and time consuming to act on a record when the agent was not in the office. Others might not know which agent's desk to search. The assistant manager came up with a compromise that met everyone's needs. She suggested that the physical records be kept at the agent's desk when in an active mode, but that a record should be entered into the computer even when no air had been booked. This way, anyone could check in the centralized computer database and immediately see which agent's desk would have the full file.

This experience demonstrates two of the points that have been discussed. One is the need to regularly review and be willing to revise policies as conditions change. The other is to make the rules realistic. Remember, once you set a policy, you have to be ready to enforce it. If the rules are not realistic, you will be unable to enforce them and, once you can't enforce a policy, subordinates will stop trusting your credibility and ability to keep the other rules in place. Once they can regularly "get away" with ignoring rules, they will push the envelope on other policies just as children do with adults!

There will still be times when one manager oversteps his or her bounds and makes a decision that should have been left for the other. In such cases, it is important that the managers remain united. They should not fight in front of the "children," but should get out of the office to discuss what must now be done. In some cases, however, it might be necessary to rescind the decision that had been made. This, too, must be a joint decision and must be presented to those involved as a final answer without room for negotiation.

It is in the nature of subordinates to try to get their way if they can, even if it means playing one parent against the other. It is the parent's job to make sure this type of game doesn't succeed.

The military maintains the ultimate "chain of command," where everyone knows exactly what everyone else is responsible for and, in fact, can get in trouble for bypassing the normal order. It can cause a real problem for subordinates in the military to try to go around their immediate superior. We do not recommend this extreme an atmosphere in a civilian office, but it doesn't hurt to learn a little from such examples. Children need to learn at an early age that, in the long run, it doesn't pay to play Mom

"We always ask Jane first."

against Dad or vice versa, and your employees need to learn the same.

Situations or requests will periodically arise that do not fit into anything already spelled out. In such cases, employees will naturally tend to go to whichever parent they believe will provide the response they want. Rather than make a hasty decision in such cases, especially if a similar situation is likely to arise again in the future, the parent so approached should take the position that no decision can be made immediately. Then, depending on the urgency of the request, the decision can either go to the next regular planning meeting of the managers or to an emergency meeting. If the request is of a moderate or higher kind of importance, the manager on site should try to contact the missing manager before rendering a decision even if a co-manager is out of town. Only if it is critical to make a decision immediately, or if it is a very minor matter, should the on-site manager provide a decision on the spot. In such cases, however, the manager should make sure to advise the missing co-manager as soon as possible so that no perception can possibly be given of an attempt to do something "behind their back."

Reconciling Differences

Many divorces are at least partially due to the inability of the spouses to agree on how to raise the children and other aspects of the joint management of the household. This is also true of divorces between partners in small businesses.

Doris

We consulted with a business owned and run by two female partners, Joan and Martha. They had been friends a long while and had decided to start the business together without really discussing who would be responsible for what and their very different attitudes towards employees.

Joan was fairly well versed in business-related areas and had been a manager in a bank previously. Martha, on the other hand, had never been in a managerial position in any business, but had been an extremely effective frontline salesperson. In the early stages, the business went well. The success of the business had hinged on their own individual work, and they really didn't have enough of a staff to cause any problems. By the time we were called in to consult with them, however, things were starting to go downhill, due primarily to their vastly different management styles and lack of willingness to understand the other's viewpoints.

By this time, they had a total staff of five—the two co-owners and three frontline salespeople. Joan, who had financial experience but no sales experience, did the bookkeeping, general office management, and some sales. Martha was primarily a salesperson.

Although Martha was a good salesperson, she had no prior supervisory experience. She believed that employees needed strict rules or they wouldn't work well. She would rarely grant a request that was at all out of the ordinary.

Joan, on the other hand, believed that they had basically good employees and that, since, in their business, they really couldn't pay high salaries, it was important to be as generous as possible with policies that wouldn't cost hard dollars. The employees quickly learned to go to Joan with any request and to try to avoid Martha. Joan was usually quite liberal in granting such requests.

By the time we were called in to help them, the office was suffering from high employee turnover, loss of customers, and a downturn in income that had thrown the business into a loss. Very quickly we realized that people (both employees and customers) were leaving primarily because of the obvious tensions between Joan and Martha.

The problem was not that one owner believed in strict rules and the other believed in more flexibility. The real problem was that they had never discussed how they would handle their staff. This situation is exactly the same as when a couple starts a family before talking about their different views on disciplining and raising children. As we'll discuss in chapter 9, neither a permissive nor an authoritarian style is specifically right or wrong—there are examples of successes and failures in families and businesses with both. However, unresolved inconsistencies between parents, home or office, almost universally cause problems. Children and subordinates pick up on it, simultaneously taking advantage of it and becoming uncomfortable because of it.

Children and employees both need to know what the rules are and what the results will be if they are broken. They need to know that this doesn't change merely due to which parent is home at the moment. The parents must get together and compromise, if necessary, on how they will raise the family. Managers must compromise where necessary on just how strict or lenient to be with employees. Both strict and lenient structures will work if everyone knows the rules and the rules are applied consistently.

Unfortunately, in the case of Joan and Martha, we were called in too late. The tensions and resentments between the partners were too strong, and the best employees had left. The economy was in a recession and the company was already too weak to survive. In effect, the co-owners agreed to a divorce and the business closed down because of their inability to agree on how to run it.

In fact, the managers were guilty of another activity that feuding parents frequently engage in. They had been using the employees to get at each other every chance they could. Due to the differences between them, even in areas beyond their supervision of their employees, they had gone from being friends to being virtual enemies. In the office, each one would accuse the other, in front of the staff, of being guilty of any transgression. They would even go out of their way looking for situations that would reinforce their growing dislike for each other. This put the employees in the middle of a fight between the managers. Nothing will tear a family apart more quickly. Parents who are divided instead of united create impossible tensions that will inevitably lead to disaster within the group.

Working with a Co-Manager with a Different Set of Values

When you can choose your co-manager, it is important to make sure that you share a similar value system. This will reduce the potential for conflict. You can choose your own co-manager when you decide to partner with someone in a business or when you promote an employee or hire a new person to become your assistant manager or co-manager. Unfortunately, it is sometimes difficult, if not impossible, to choose your own co-manager. If your boss has promoted someone to be your assistant or co-manager and has not consulted you or has rejected your suggestions, you may be stuck with someone who has values vastly different from yours. The best advice is to sit down with the new co-manager and discuss these differences openly to determine precisely what your combined culture will be and who will be responsible for what. If this is not done in the very beginning, you will be guaranteeing disruptive disputes later on.

Do not agree on a "let's wait until it happens" plan. However, be careful to enter this discussion with an open mind and an expectation of mutual cooperation and willingness to compromise. There is no such thing as a "winner" in these cases. Both parties are either losers or both become winners because they work well together as a team for the good of all.

Donald

When we sold one of our businesses to a division of another company, I became the vice-president in charge of all operations of this division. The two people who had formerly been running the operations now reported to me. We never really agreed on much of anything. We tried to make it work, but the differences were at times just too much to bridge. In the end, it was a contributing factor to the frustrations that caused me to look elsewhere.

On the flip side, a few years earlier, I had been promoted to manage a project and was working for someone who also tended to approach things very differently than I do. In this case, however, we were able to discuss and devise a set of responsibilities and authorities that left me free to manage as I saw fit, as long as certain schedule and cost guidelines were met. We literally wrote out our respective responsibilities in two columns on the same page. Whenever one of us was becoming uncomfortable with the other, we referred back to that agreement. It solved a lot of problems!

If you ever do find yourself in this situation, make sure that you and your co-manager work together and present the united front already discussed. If you do, you have a chance at the success that Donald experienced in the latter situation. It doesn't guarantee success, as the former situation proved; however, if you never try to address the differences directly, you will find yourself in the Joan/Martha scenario and your team will suffer. This does not mean that one of you must give in on your principles, but it does mean that you need to negotiate a compromise in some areas. Compromise does not mean win/lose. Each party gives a little for the ultimate benefit of the overall office. Your staff will respect both of you more when you show that, despite different styles, you can work together for the benefit of the team.

Competition Between Co-Parents

Another similar problem in families and offices is the tendency for co-managers to compete with each other for their employees' affection. Insecure parents and managers find themselves falling into this trap. Your children do not have to like you every minute, and it doesn't really matter which parent they "like" better. In the end, they will respect parents who act like parents and who show that they are not afraid to stand up for what is right.

Employees may "like" a person who always gives them their way out of fear of rejection, but they will not respect or work as hard for that person and will not feel secure themselves about what to expect in the office. A parent who can't take the occasional "I hate you" from a child isn't an effective parent. Sometimes, you need to know what is best for your child even when the child sees it differently. You also are charged with the responsibility of doing what is best for the entire family. If you cannot take an employee's being mad at you, even if only temporarily, then don't seek a managerial or ownership position.

Keep in mind that consistently enforcing rules does not mean forbidding disagreements from subordinates. Employees should always feel free and safe about suggesting changes in policies. However, changes should not be made impulsively just to please a given employee or set of employees. When an employee or group of employees does voice an objection to a policy or make a suggestion for change, managers should think of the advice given in *Parenting for Dummies.*

When you encourage your kids to express their differing points of view, you are doing the following:
—helping your children to explain their feelings
—encouraging discussions
—allowing your children to be heard
—teaching fairness

The same holds true in the office. It is important to encourage employees to express and explain their feelings. They may have some very good points the managers haven't considered that might result in a change of policy. Even if their suggestions are not accepted, they will understand, if they feel they have been heard and if the reasons for rejecting their ideas are explained to them logically. It is always healthy to encourage discussion, since the more employees feel there is two-way communication within the office, the better they will accept some policies that are not exactly to their liking.

When managers listen to their subordinates and accept some valid suggestions, the employees learn that the office is run fairly. They understand that decisions are not made impulsively or emotionally and that their managers are open-minded and willing to change if given logical reasons for doing so. They tolerate differences of view better themselves and ultimately perform better.

When you, as one of the managers, are asked about a policy and you do not know or do not remember what the correct answer is, don't be afraid to admit that you aren't sure. Promise to check with your co-manager and get back to the employee within a reasonable time. Then, do so.

The best security blanket a child can have is parents who respect each other.
—Jan Blaustone
The Joy of Parenthood

Tips from Managers

1. Back up a co-manager even if he or she promised something different from what you would have promised.

2. Do not make decisions that are not your responsibility to make.

3. Coordinate authority areas with each other.

4. Review and revise policies as necessary.

5. Enforce policies or change them.

6. Meet with co-managers regularly—away from the staff—in a relaxed time and place.

7. Do not make hasty decisions in non-emergency situations.

8. Accept that you and a co-manager can have differing opinions and viewpoints, yet be willing to compromise.

9. Do not talk to employees about your problems with a co-manager.

10. Do not compete with a co-manager.

Tips from Employees

1. Let us know clearly who is responsible for what so we don't get confused about which manager to go to. Please put this in writing in a company manual.

2. Expect us to go to the manager we feel most likely to grant our wish unless you have made it clear to us who is responsible for that area.

3. Know your own office's policies. Don't let us feel that we know them better than you do.

4. Be open and let us know that we won't get in trouble if we bring conflicts to our manager's attention in a respectful, constructive way. Perhaps, provide a place where we can anonymously let you know about such conflicts.

5. Work together with your co-managers so we don't get caught between you.

6. If you and a co-manager disagree on something, let us know how you both feel, but let us know what the policy for the company will be.

7. Do not complain to us about a co-manager. This just makes us feel uncomfortable. Work it out together without involving us.

8. When discussing something with your co-manager(s) that might be controversial, please do so after hours or outside the office. Even when we know you are friends, we don't like to hear you argue.

9. Do not compete with each other for our loyalty. We work for all our managers and can't afford to show favoritism for one over another.

10. Make decisions based on what is "right," not on how you can beat your co-manager.

PART II

Proven Parenting Techniques Every Manager Should Master

CHAPTER 8

Realize That Each Child Is Different: Maximize Each Person's Strengths and Minimize Their Weaknesses

When it comes to people and their quirks, idiosyncrasies, and personality flaws, the variety seems to be limitless. The manager's aim always remains the same: to keep these human beings from clogging up the workings of their group.

—Andrew S. Grove
CEO of Intel Corporation, as quoted in
One-On-One With Andy Grove

Doris
Three peanut butter and jelly sandwiches—how difficult could that be? Well, if you're a parent with more than one child, you know. One child wanted nutty peanut butter with grape jelly, the second wanted smooth peanut butter with grape jelly, while the third wanted smooth peanut butter with strawberry jelly. And God forbid if we got it wrong.

What do peanut butter and jelly sandwiches have to do with management? It demonstrates the need to balance the differences of each person and treat them appropriately.

Our family was no different than any other with three kids. While they shared many personality characteristics, they were all quite different. As any parent knows, these differences can be the cause of the vast majority of stress in the family.

Doris and Phil
Donald excelled academically and, as the oldest child, tended to feel that he knew best. Doug was the social one, who would introduce himself

123

and get along with almost anyone. As Donald's younger brother, he (of course) sought to find out whatever Donald thought and emphatically disagree with him. Dana, the youngest, was the family athlete. You name the sport and she would excel at it. All three of them expressed their feelings in very different ways. Throw in the two parents and you had quite a group.

We, of course, had the typical difficulties of balancing these differences. If either Doug or Dana had been compared to Donald academically, or Donald and Doug had been expected to do as well as Dana in sports, we would have had a disaster! Our job was to make each of our children feel good and help them each excel in their areas of strength without making the others feel inferior.

Our office was no different. At one point, we had a very young woman who was still living at home and for whom this was the first office job, a divorced gentleman whose kids lived hundreds of miles away, a working wife whose husband was pressuring her to spend more time with their two-year-old, and a middle-aged woman whose kids had long since left the nest. And this was just a small business—imagine the differences that exist in larger corporations.

If Andy Grove were famous for parenting instead of business advice, the quote at the beginning of the chapter would read:

> When it comes to **children** and their quirks, idiosyncrasies, and personality flaws, the variety seems to be limitless. The **parent's** aim always remains the same: to keep these human beings from clogging up the workings of their **family.**

In thirty years of running our businesses and consulting with others, we've always said that managing would be easy if it wasn't for all the people. Variety may be the spice of life, but when it comes to managing it is also a never-ending source of stress. If everyone reacted to praise, prodding, and punishment the same way, everything would be much simpler.

Virtually all parenting experts agree that, since each child is different, parents must teach, encourage, and punish each differently. But what does that mean to office families?

In *Parenting for Dummies,* Sandra Hardin Gookin warns parents not to be tempted to teach their children by comparing one sibling to another or even to themselves. It is important, she notes, for parents to keep this warning in mind when they create expectations or goals for their children. Parents must consider each child separately and accept that child for whatever that child is. It doesn't matter if one sibling walked early, talked early, or even learned to ride a bike more easily. Each one will learn in his or her own time.

We have found this advice works equally well in business. We tend to be much less forgiving with adults than we are with children, but everyone needs time and space to learn and perform in their own way. We have had several employees over the years who were fast learners and others who took much more time and assistance to learn new skills. However, once they each learned the skills, all of them were productive, excellent employees who were assets to our company. One way to prevent problems is, when hiring a new employee, not to concentrate only on what is needed today. You must look to the future and the expected growth of the position and hire people who have that capacity for growth and flexibility. People don't stop learning when childhood ends as they did in the past; today, everyone has to continue learning new skills throughout their careers.

Parents have the responsibility to bring out the best in all their children and help them grow to be productive members of society. Doing so with more than one child requires an understanding of how the children differ from each other and which tactics work best for each child. The office is no different. Good managers set their employees up for success, not failure. They understand how their employees differ and what to do to help them grow and function effectively together despite, perhaps even because of, those differences.

What Are Some Differences Offices Encounter?

1. Office "kids" have different strengths and weaknesses. In many homes, parents have found that automatically assigning the same chores to each child, with each taking his or her turn on certain days or weeks, leads to unhappy children. Instead, they let each child do what he or she does best and enjoys most. Those chores that no one really wants to do or that several want to do get shared. With this method, the chores are performed better and everyone is happier.

Just because Raymond is a boy doesn't mean he has to mow the lawn if he hates it and his sister, Susan, enjoys it. And Raymond, who loves to cook, can take more turns helping cook dinner than his sister.

This can work incredibly well in your office. The first step in getting the right person for the right job is in hiring the "right" person. However, as any manager who has ever hired employees knows, what the resume and interview seem to reflect can vary quite substantially from reality.

In several cases we hired a person with a particular role in mind. Rather quickly, we discovered that the person lacked some of the necessary skills for what we had planned.

Doris

Many years ago we hired a woman, Diane, to be a coordinator of group travel, a position involving a great deal of detail and paperwork. We quickly discovered, however, that Diane was not very good with details and with following up on the necessary paperwork. However, we did find out that she was wonderful in working with people who were either inquiring about the trips or had already booked.

Rather than firing her because she wasn't exactly right for the job description we had in mind, we changed the parameters of the position. We put her in charge of working with the group participants, both those booked and those who were just prospects, and had another staff member work on the necessary follow-up paperwork. By doing this, we probably substantially increased the number of people who purchased the trips and everyone was happy and well placed for their skills.

In another case, we had hired a woman, Millie, as a receptionist/secretary. Again, however, we found that Millie was not particularly good at the detail work essential for a good secretary. But, just as with Diane, she was wonderful with people. We moved her over to a travel-agent position and moved another employee into the secretarial position. Millie went on to become our top salesperson for many years.

What is the solution when you have hired good people, but they have skills that are not exactly right for the position for which they were hired? You can just fire them and replace them with someone new. After all, in the cases described above, the employees clearly turned out not to possess the skill set we thought their resumes, experience, and interviews indicated. Getting rid of them may seem a simple solution, but "raising an office" in the most effective way is rarely that simple. Should we have tried to work with them to improve their attention to detail? Nice thought, but that would have been like running up a very steep hill. The problem was, if you were the leader of one of our travel groups, you wouldn't have wanted Diane to be responsible for your group. She just couldn't do it accurately, and any effort to the contrary would be trying to force a square peg into a round hole.

What other choices did we have?

Observing these supposedly "bad hires" objectively, we found that customers who called about taking the trips and people already booked into the groups just loved talking with Diane, and people calling the office responded very well to Millie. Their sales skills and ability to keep customers happy were very strong. We opted against wasting a lot of training and supervision only to get, at best, a moderately successful group operations coordinator or a barely adequate receptionist.

Instead, we redefined the focus of their jobs, making them the primary contact person for prospects and participants, and had someone else who was good with details, but not as good with people, take over the detail tasks. The result—for the several years both of these women worked with us—was that we had a superb group sales manager with many successful and profitable groups and a topnotch travel agent.

The other employee, whose job was also redefined, had been a mediocre salesperson. Now relieved of some of those tasks, she became a very efficient operations coordinator. Instead of two marginally successful employees, both of whom would have been only moderately happy with their jobs, we had two successful people, both happy with what they were doing and both highly productive for the office. The company made more money with both jobs performed more effectively because we looked at the strengths and weaknesses of each individual and responded appropriately.

Some of our greatest consulting successes have come in teaching others how to implement these principles.

Doris and Phil

We recently consulted with a store that had each salesperson take the next customer in turn, regardless of who or what the customer wanted or what type of customer it was. They were only moderately successful in meeting sales quotas. When we convinced them to start setting some criteria on who took what type of customer where possible, their sales increased substantially. Obviously, not all customers could be categorized, so many were still taken in turn. However, we found that one salesperson was especially effective with young, twenty-something-type customers, while another, older gentleman was great with sixty-plus customers. A third salesperson, who had come from the South himself, was wonderful with people who obviously came from the South. They would identify with each other immediately.

Salespeople were trained, when greeting a new prospect, to determine if they fit a "specialist" category and, if they did, to introduce them to the "specialist." The list of "specialists" was in writing, and an effort was made to keep it fair so that all salespeople would have some specialties. When the store implemented this program, after some initial discomfort, not only did sales go up, but the salespeople were happier as well.

*"This is Carl. One of his weaknesses is that
he's always talking about his strengths."*

In fact, varied personalities within a company enable the business to work well with the varied personalities and needs of customers. If you are having a personality conflict between a customer and an employee, the best solution is to let another employee with a different, more compatible, personality help the customer. This is not necessarily a poor reflection on the first employee; it is merely a recognition that some personalities get along together better than others.

A manager who remains flexible, instead of rigidly insisting that everyone do what the manager originally perceived as the job description, will ultimately create a staff that works effectively as a team and that respects the strengths and weaknesses of each member.

2. Different personalities exist among office "kids." Children have many different personalities. One may be shy; another is outgoing or, even, domineering. Neither personality trait is inherently good or bad unless it interferes with the growth of the child.

If your office has members who are natural leaders, like Anne, whom we discussed in chapter 2, make sure you work with them to help them lead their co-workers in the right direction. Otherwise, they may become the chief complainers and bring out everyone's petty little grievances. Very often, the chronic complainer is a leader in disguise. An infectious personality is an asset when it works for you, but it can destroy an office, or a family, if it is allowed to run free.

Offices need varied kinds of personalities. Remember Barbara, from chapter 3, whom we promoted to office manager over two other more senior employees? Because her strengths were different from those of her co-workers, she earned that position and allowed us to focus on marketing, finance, strategic planning, and other management functions instead of day-to-day operations. The entire company benefited because we recognized that her personality traits made her "right" for the manager position, and the personalities of her co-workers made them good for their jobs but not for manager.

3. Family members learn in different ways. Good parents or managers make sure that all of the people for whom they are responsible are provided with the best learning environments and opportunities available within their budget. Some people learn quickly; others take more time, but once they learn something, you can count on them to follow what they've been taught. Some people can watch how something is done once and repeat the action themselves effortlessly. Others have to see it several times, then do it themselves under close supervision, and, finally, can be set loose to do it on their own.

Doris

In our office, we've always done most of the training in-house. We have computer-based instruction for some things, training videos or manuals for others. Since we are professional trainers, we often design and conduct our own training. However, we had one employee several years ago who just didn't learn well from these informal methods.

We found that a five-day course was available for her to learn the primary computer program our travel agency used and, since we knew she would learn best from a structured class, we sent her. It worked very well. She came back confident and able to use the system. Most other new employees preferred working at their own pace within the office and learning as they needed it. It's important to remember that there is no "right" or "wrong" way to teach someone, as long as it works.

This same employee, by the way, also needed formal, regular evaluations of her work. Being a small office where everyone knew each other very well, we did not have a systematized program of annual or semi-annual evaluations. We evaluated people as we went along. However, we found that this employee needed to specifically be told that she was doing her job properly and that we approved, so we set up semi-annual written evaluations for her.

If you do something like this, make sure you make it available to any other employees who would like it. In our case, the rest of the staff was perfectly happy not to bother with formal evaluations.

Just as you might choose different schools or other learning activities for different children within the same family, you need to choose different training methods to bring out the best in your employees. Some do best with formalized training, some with simple instructions, and others with a combination of demonstration and working under supervision.

With each type of person, regardless of the kind of training you choose, it is important to let them know what end result is expected. Be specific. We once read about a professional football player who was asked why he fell on a fumble rather than run it back for a touchdown when the field in front of him was wide open. He responded, "My contract gives me a bonus for fumble recoveries. It says nothing about running them back." That's an excellent example of what can happen when you give incentives for the wrong end result.

The biggest mistake managers make is trying to teach everyone by the methods that work best for the managers themselves. As a manager, your job is to learn how your employees learn and work to provide the right situation for them.

Doris
In our family, when Donald was babysitting for his brother and sister and was old enough to make dinner for all of them, we merely left verbal instructions with him about what to make for dinner and how to make it. On the other hand, a friend of ours needed to leave complete written instructions, outlining all steps involved, for her son when he was left in charge of his younger siblings. He was insecure without such detailed information.

4. Different people respond to discipline differently.

Doris
When Doug was in the fourth grade, his teacher was having some problems with him. She asked our permission to keep him in the classroom with her during recess. She knew he loved recess and was sure if he were deprived of it he would correct his behavior. We warned her that we

didn't think this would work, even though it did with most children. From our experience, we believed that he would love the one-on-one attention from the teacher. However, we welcomed her attempt. After two weeks of trying this, Doug's teacher called and told us that it wasn't working. She was amazed, but he just loved that half-hour with her complete attention.

There are employees like this as well, who will "misbehave" to get attention.

When you have someone whom you believe is creating situations for attention, make sure that you correct their behavior very quickly and don't let them monopolize your time. Put quick notes of correction on their work and send it back. Try not to get into long discussions. Have another experienced employee show them the "correct" way to do something, so they do not always get a manager's attention. Give them less attention and more praise when they are right.

Parenting for Dummies works as well in the office as it does in the home. The author, Sandra Hardin Gookin, points out the difference between discipline and punishment. "Discipline is all about setting ground rules and boundaries—and making your [office] children live and follow those rules." Punishment is the penalty inflicted when those rules and boundaries are violated. She suggests several rules to follow in meting out punishment.

1. Make the punishment fit the crime.

2. Be realistic when setting the punishment.

3. Don't be too lenient.

4. Make the punishment a learning exercise.

5. Consider your punishment carefully.

The key, she says, is consistency and follow-through, which is exactly what we have seen work in the office "family" as well.

5. Different people react to praise differently. Some children need regular reassurance that they are pleasing their parents. This is true even after they become adults. These employees are usually somewhat insecure. They will tend to ask for approval if it doesn't come spontaneously. Make sure to give these employees a frequent "pat on the back" when they do good work. However, don't forget to give such pats to your other employees as well. It is very easy to think of the "squeaky wheel" and forget those loyal employees who don't "squeak" as much. People who say they don't need praise are lying. Everyone appreciates being told they are doing a good job; and ultimately anyone will feel under-appreciated if long periods go by without receiving praise. It's true with children, and it's true with your office family as well.

Remember the case in chapter 3 of Connie, the teenager who appeared to be so mature and confident and whose mother depended on her for much assistance with her younger siblings? Her mother assumed that Connie realized how much she appreciated her help, but didn't verbalize it to Connie. After Connie had run away from home, her mother was shocked to find out how much Connie had misunderstood her mother's appreciation, since Connie was definitely her favorite child. We brought them back together and, once her mother verbalized how she felt, Connie had a whole different perspective and came home happily.

Don't forget your employees who don't ask for praise—they still need it. You may lose them if you ignore them and, unlike Connie's mother, you won't get a second chance for them to "come home." It's up to the managers to remember that everyone needs to know they're important.

6. Different positions within the office family are given different privileges. In home families, an older child has certain privileges that are not extended to younger siblings, and the baby of the family will be allowed to "get away" with some things that an older sibling will not. Office families, too, display differences based on position.

An experienced employee who has been with the company for a long time will be given more leeway to do things independently, may get more vacation days, etc. Things such as additional vacation days or other specific privileges that come with tenure should be spelled out in a policy manual. Privileges such as greater independence to decide how to do something are not in writing—they come naturally as the person shows the maturity and ability to perform independently. This is OK, as long as the "bene's" don't interfere with the focus of the organization and don't negatively impact the functionality of everyone else in the office.

7. Different people have different work ethics. In today's business world, people come to the office with very different priorities. A couple of generations ago, workers (generally men) were expected to put their jobs first. If overtime was needed, the worker stayed late. If the company wanted the employee to move to another city, the family made the move. The rest of the family made the necessary sacrifices for the breadwinner.

Times have changed, creating another source of conflict in many

companies. Some workers are as dedicated to the job as in past generations, while others, although capable workers, do not consider their job
their first priority. Their family, or even their own free time, may come
first. If their child is in a soccer game this evening, they will leave the
office to attend the game even if a project is not finished. This is very
hard for some managers to accept. They consider the worker disloyal
and get very resentful of the employee's attitude.

In our consulting, we have had to teach many business owners and
managers that they cannot judge an employee by their own work-ethic
standards. As long as employees are providing effective results during the
time for which they are being paid, we cannot judge them poorly for putting their family first. Everyone has the right to set their own personal priorities.

It is fair, however, when it comes time for promotion to managerial
positions to take an employee's priorities into consideration. Since management carries with it a greater responsibility to make sure things are
done, there may be a need to pass over a good employee who has to leave
the office at five or who cannot come in on a weekend to finish something. This does not mean we do not like the person or even admire their
abilities, but flexibility of time is needed if they want to get into management. A business does have to protect its own interests, while trying to
provide as much flexibility to employees for other priorities as well.
Employees, on the other hand, must realize that they can't have it all. They
have to make choices and set priorities. That being said, in times like
today where finding and keeping skilled talent is one of our biggest challenges, it is incumbent on the business to help structure jobs (both in management and on the frontline) to fit in well with one's personal life. In our
time managing and consulting, we've found that the most effective people at all levels are ones who live balanced lives.

Workaholics tend to expect everyone else to be like them. When they
are mixed with non-workaholics, great resentment can occur in the staff,
who have no interest in that level of commitment. You have to judge each
person's performance based on what is expected at that position. This is
no different from insisting that our children do their chores and finish
their homework as long as they have been assigned a reasonable amount
of responsibility that could be expected to be finished on time.

The 1960s and 1970s brought about clichés such as "do your own
thing" and "different strokes for different folks." Managers were expected to recognize the differences among workers and act appropriately. We

have always expected parents to recognize and accept the differences among their children, but we have not always expected the same in the workplace. In the past, workers were expected to adapt their needs to the workplace. Today, the workplace has to adapt to the varying needs of employees, or the business won't attract the people it needs to move forward.

To do this effectively, we must keep the lines of communication open between workers and managers and encourage workers to be open to each other. Managers must keep their antennae up constantly to become aware of potential problems before they become crises.

Differences among workers can lead to major challenges in business if we do not continually make the effort to help our employees work together as a family, respecting each other for who and what they each are and helping each other meet the ultimate needs of their company.

Why We Like Some Employees More (or Less) Than Others

We are not immune to the effects and biases of our own past experiences. It is normal for a parent to like one child more (or less) than another. Which one is liked more or less can vary with the situation. The same is true for managers. The challenge for both parents and managers is to keep these likes and dislikes from being too obvious and to avoid, as much as is humanly possible, making decisions based on these biases.

Parents tend to favor the child who mirrors their traits or those of others whom they like and enjoy, and resent and even dislike at times the child who exhibits traits they dislike. We carry these same prejudices as managers.

As the office "parents," managers must fight hard, first to recognize their biases for what they are and then to look beyond them in judging an employee. Is the employee's work and contribution adequate or is he or she truly disrupting the effectiveness of the office? If the honest answer to this is that the office is doing fine and we are the ones who are annoyed, then we must overcome our dislike of the traits shown and look only at the work performed. This is not as easy as it sounds, but a good manager must be able to rise above personal biases in working with employees.

The thing that impresses me most about America is the way parents obey their children.   —Duke of Windsor

Tips from Managers

1. Understand that employees come to you with different backgrounds, personalities, and priorities. Accept them for who they are, not for who you want them to be.

2. Personalities within the office will differ. Some will be outgoing and assertive; some will be quiet and even withdrawn. Help them work together as a team, bringing out the best in both.

3. Your employees will have varying strengths and weaknesses. Work to maximize the strengths and minimize the weaknesses of each of your employees.

4. Use an appropriate style of training for each person; don't expect them all to learn best in the same way. Be creative to help them do their best.

5. Use appropriate discipline for each. Make sure that any punishment fits the crime.

6. Use appropriate levels of praise for each individual. Be sure to give praise even to those employees who appear to need it least.

7. Remember that personality conflicts will arise from time to time. They could be between co-workers, between an employee and a manager, or between a customer and an employee. Don't judge who is "right" or "wrong." Just find a way to accomplish the goals that all share.

8. Don't judge others' priorities by your own. Judge only the work that is being done in view of the position and ambitions of the worker.

9. Don't compare one employee with another. One may learn more slowly than another but, once having learned, be just as valuable an employee.

10. Above all, keep all lines of communication open.

Tips from Employees

1. Don't compare me with my co-workers. We are all different and should be valued for ourselves.

2. Try to find the best training opportunities for me, based on my strengths and weaknesses. I want to learn, but I am not just like my co-workers or you.

3. Be patient with me if I take longer to learn a new skill. Once I learn it, I will perform effectively.

4. If I am not exactly what you thought you hired, try to work with me. Slight restructuring of my job description might give both of us an advantage. Please be flexible.

5. Try to work with us to bring out our best and minimize our weaknesses. Help us form teams where we can help each other.

6. Remember that I do not necessarily have the same priorities as you or some of my co-workers. They might not have to get home right after work, while I must pick my children up immediately. I will give you my best during my working hours, but I have responsibilities outside of the office that are important to me. If I cannot work late, it is not because I don't care—it is because I have other critical responsibilities.

7. It's normal for you to like some of us more than others, but please look beyond your feelings when judging our work.

8. When we do something wrong, please don't overreact. Let the punishment fit our "crime" and help us learn from our mistakes.

9. Promote us based on our abilities or our contribution to the company, not just for how long we have been here.

10. Just because I don't ask for praise doesn't mean I don't ever need it. We all need to know we're important.

CHAPTER 9

Don't Be a Pushover or "Pal" Parent:
Let Their Peers Be Their Pals

Sometimes we try so hard to be a kid's pal, we forget to be their parent. . . .
Pals, they got—parents, they need.   —Kelsey Grammer
               in an NBC public service announcement

Doris and Phil

One small business that was a consulting client of ours was having a high rate of turnover and constant challenges with their staff. The business was owned and managed by Claudia, a woman who wanted everyone to like her. She most enjoyed selling to customers and basically abdicated most management functions. For many years, the business had been moderately profitable and Claudia sat back taking for granted that as long as she was successful at selling, the business would run itself. After all, her three employees were mature, experienced adults, so they shouldn't need much managing.

Unfortunately, as we know, that is not true. As the business climate became more challenging, Claudia began to experience the problems that had been there all along, but that good times had covered up.

Claudia violated many of the suggestions we have been talking about so far. She had no written policies, made decisions on the spur of the moment depending on how she was feeling at the time, and expected her staff to all pitch in and help each other without any real supervision. She literally expected the office to run itself.

She hated to say no to any employee for fear they would be "mad" at her, and she avoided setting any rules. When someone made a mistake, she would fix it.

Two years before she called us, two of her longtime employees retired. She hired two new, younger people who had a few years' experience but were not of the same temperament as the "old" staff. However, Claudia still tried the same "pal" type of supervision that had been in place before. This mismanagement, or lack of management, resulted in complete turnover of staff during the second year and a dangerous decline in profitability, which was why she called on us for help.

We ultimately convinced her to continue the selling functions that she loved, but to hire an office manager. The new manager was responsible for overseeing the staff while Claudia continued to bring in new business. Over the next year, the office was brought back to reasonable profitability and all employees were more secure and happy.

We've all been at the restaurant or mall and seen it—kids who are out of control and misbehaving. They're sending all the signals that they need to be given guidelines for behavior, but the parents just aren't getting it. Maybe the parents are not paying attention because they are too caught up in their own world. Worse, they may see the behavior but laugh it off as being cute, or they think it is undesirable to restrain the "natural" behavior of children. The child notices this positive reinforcement and is encouraged to do even more. Worse still, maybe the parents just don't care. In this case, the children continue to push the boundaries further and further to get attention or just to see how much they can get away with.

This same behavior plays itself out in the office. Managers who are too caught up in their own work act like the first example above; managers who are too permissive are the second; and those who simply don't care are similar to the third.

Running an office is tough. As managers, we have to find the right mix. We must keep our professional distance from the employees who work for us, yet still be personal. If we really care about them, we can't help but want to be close. If we like them, we have a social need for friendship just as they do. We are put in the role of judge and jury and need to be credible; but just as importantly, we need to be supportive and nurturing (and some of us probably find the confrontation inherent in doling out "punishment" distasteful and uncomfortable).

We really want everyone to get along and play by the rules, and we often react to breaches of those rules in quick and arbitrary ways. We may even intentionally "unintentionally" look the other way. Donald used to referee soccer, and the one thing he found that always quieted an angry coach or player was telling them, "Hey, number 12 was blocking my view, so I didn't see the play." Everyone knows referees can only call what they see! There is always the temptation to avoid uncomfortable conflict by ignoring what you see and rationalizing that you didn't really see it.

Parents face similar challenges daily. We can learn from good parenting techniques what we should be doing in our role as office parent. Most parents want to get along with their children. However, parents who are too easy or too close to their kids risk losing their ability to effectively prepare their children for the world ahead of them. Office "parents" who are pushovers may feel they have a close relationship with their employees, but it is not based on the mutual respect required for getting performance from their staff, and it is not healthy.

The balance is a difficult one at work and at home. Donald, who is usually an effective leader at work, once had a rude awakening to a difference in his behavior at home.

Donald

I was preparing for the first trip I was going to take alone with my older daughter, Erika. We had lived in Atlanta for about a year, and we were

"Okay, it's agreed. We tell Lucy she's trying too hard to be a pal to the employees. But we wait until after she takes us out for ice cream."

going back to Maryland to visit the family. Daria, our younger daughter, was less than a year old, so my wife and I decided she (my wife) would stay home with Daria, and Erika and I would make it a father/daughter trip.

The night before we were leaving, Erika told my wife that she was really looking forward to the trip with Daddy. Yvonne asked Erika why she was looking forward to it so much, expecting a simple reply about how much fun it would be. Instead, much to my surprise, the answer was, "It's gonna be fun 'cause Daddy never says no."

With a four-year-old, this attitude (or, more appropriately, Donald's behavior that led to the attitude) can be quickly corrected. If, however, Donald had earned this reputation with his employees, it would likely have seriously challenged the effectiveness and cohesiveness of his team.

Permissive or Strict?

In her book, *The Winning Family,* Dr. Louise Hart describes permissive as one of the three basic discipline styles. Permissive parents "abdicate power and there are often no rules, limits or structure," she says. "The result is parents who feel discouraged, confused and angry, and powerless with children who feel out of control, unloved, and low self-esteem."

Alan and Robert Davidson, in *How Good Parents Raise Great Kids,* go so far as to say that the most pervasive parenting style is permissive, perhaps because it is the path of least resistance and gives parents a false sense that the children love them. They say, and we agree, that whatever the reason, this should be avoided at all costs. Their review of the expert literature results in the bold, but accurate, statement: *The less quality disciplining a child receives, the more likely he is to grow up unloving and disrespectful.*

Managers are continually complaining about the poor teamwork skills and attitudes younger workers bring to the workforce today. Much of this is the result of the overly permissive approach parents take at home. When managers continue this all-too-common "abdicratic" style of abdicating managerial responsibility, they reinforce their employees' view of the nature and role of the parent/child relationship whether at home or at work. The results are rarely positive for either the quality of work or the job satisfaction of both the office parent and the office child.

We've seen examples of children and workers with permissive parents and managers who still lead productive lives and professional careers. Usually, however, when we look closely at these situations, we find some of these critical elements.

1. The "child" (whether the young kid at home or the subordinate at work) has natural self-initiative and self-discipline tendencies.

2. There is a common understanding that, while the "child" has great leeway, there is a fundamental line that cannot be crossed. It may look like a completely open environment, but there are certain basic rules that are not violated.

3. Whether from internal drive of the "child" or the natural leadership and charisma of the "parent," the "children" want to succeed for themselves and for their "parents."

The simple fact is that while a permissive style can succeed, it clearly does not provide the highest probability of success across the greatest number of managers and employees. There is no cause/effect relationship between permissiveness and success. If anything, these successful permissive parents and managers are the exceptions that prove the rule.

So if pure leniency is not a good approach, does that mean that authoritarian rule is best? Is strict setting and enforcement of rules the best way to guarantee success in most situations? These different parental styles have long been a subject of discussion among parenting experts, and we find that their thoughts directly mirror "parenting the office" issues. No less an authority on parenting than Dr. Spock speaks of lenient versus strict parenting. "Some parents who incline towards strictness assume that their approach is a guarantee of good behavior in their children and that leniency will surely produce undisciplined, rude offspring. Both of these beliefs are mistaken—or at best only partly true."

Dr. Spock talks about how parents who are strict because of "unusually high standards" (e.g., with respect to courtesy, punctuality, helpfulness, etc.) but are basically loving can be very successful parents. But those who are strict in the sense of being overbearing and driven by a need to coerce and control will find that their domineering ways often backfire.

Dr. Don Dinkmeyer and Dr. Gary McKay, in their book *Raising a Responsible Child* and in their materials in their STEP (Systematic Training for Effective Parenting) programs, echo these same thoughts. They describe autocratic parents as leaders who disrespect their children, make all the decisions, and take responsibility for all problems. In contrast, permissive parents are leaders who disrespect themselves, let the children do what they want, and take on all the children's problems in a subservient way. While some parents luck into raising well-balanced children anyway (and some managers luck into a good staff despite either approach), it seems obvious that these approaches are not likely to work most of the time.

If leniency and strictness aren't in and of themselves good or bad—it depends on how they are applied—then where does that leave us? Must we choose whichever we perceive to be the lesser of two evils and live with the consequences?

Dr. Spock concludes that strictness versus leniency isn't the vital choice so many people make it out to be. He realized this when he discussed a much more relevant issue in parenting styles: authoritarian versus democratic styles. Authoritarian parents are mistrustful. They have a basic belief that, when left to their own devices, children will misbehave. They command and coerce. This is very similar to the age-old "Theory X" management style. Theory X managers believe that their employees are inherently lazy and untrustworthy, so they must control and coerce to get the job done. They can be task-effective, but they usually burn through people and have trouble succeeding at anything other than crisis management.

Democratic parents are the opposite. They trust their children. They understand their kids need a great deal of guidance, but they share the decision-making process, and they continue to grant authority for self-governing as the children grow and demonstrate the responsibility to handle it. This is similar to the "Theory Y" management style, which believes that most people are naturally motivated to perform and succeed. It becomes the manager's job, then, to create an environment for success and to nurture, coach, and guide employees to success. This doesn't mean that these managers are always quiet and nice. To the contrary, any of us who have participated in competitive sports know that coaches can be quite demanding. Donald remembers one of his coaches from his youth soccer days.

Donald

I had a coach who loved the players on the team and took a particular liking to me. After a few games, however, he was very frustrated with a lack of ball-control improvement. He decided that all the players would have to demonstrate the ability to juggle the ball (i.e., keep it in the air by foot or knee) at least ten times.

I was not much of an athlete and could barely keep it alive for two or three touches. This coach didn't care, and he made that clear—everyone had to do it if they wanted to play. I complained to Mom and Dad that this wasn't fair since it was an intramural league in which everyone was supposed to play, but they had no sympathy either and told me I couldn't protest if I didn't try. I was upset at what appeared to me to be an arbitrary rule made in anger and against the spirit of the league.

I liked the coach, though, so rather than stay angry myself, I decided to take it as a challenge. I practiced long and hard. Not only did I make the required ten, but I actually performed the third-longest juggle on the team.

The new skill and increased confidence made me a better player, and I realized that self-improvement really was what the league was about. Even after the exercise was no longer required, I continued to practice and improve to the point I could juggle 100 or more times. To this day, I feel a certain pride when I juggle a soccer ball.

I learned that sometimes it takes a push from someone who knows you can succeed to get you to realize your potential, and I've tried to put that lesson to use at work as well.

We agree with Dr. Spock that the real issue in the home (and the office) has never been strict versus lenient per se. Sometimes strict is the right way to go; sometimes lenient is best. But there is a difference between being fair in the application of leniency and being a pushover parent. All parenting experts agree that a *democratic leadership style* is the most effective one at home, and we extend that same judgment to office families.

By democratic, we don't mean that decisions are made by taking a vote. To do so would invite anarchy in home and office alike. We do, however, mean several things.

1. The democratic family is based on mutual respect. People may not be equal in rank, but they are all equal under the law. We once heard a story about a successful venture capitalist who would visit businesses seeking his investment before scheduling formal meetings. If he saw reserved parking spaces for the CEO and other senior executives, he simply left and never scheduled an appointment. He felt that high-growth companies depended on everyone working together, and arbitrary perks indicated a hierarchical structure lacking a foundation of mutual respect, which maximizes chances for success.

2. There is a set of defined rules and standards. Those who meet and exceed the standards excel. Those who don't are given remedial attention. Donald once worked at a company that was struggling a little bit with its consistency, and he noticed that the place was almost devoid of office lore relating to standards.

Donald

It was the strangest thing. Everywhere I've worked or consulted, there have always been stories about who the heroes of the company are and why they are so respected (just think of Lee Iacocca at Chrysler or Bill Gates at Microsoft). Similarly, there's always a tale about the person or persons who crossed the line of some organizational norm and what happened to them. They're sort of like the heads on pikes that the authorities in the Middle Ages put up on London Bridge to warn people of the consequences of violating local norms.

This place, however, had virtually no such stories. There were many excellent people, but unless you worked with them, you got no exposure to what made them successful. And while I never wish ill upon anybody, there were no stories about anyone who crossed the line. The company was more than fifteen years old, yet it had no real warning posts or guidelines. I later realized that one of the challenges the company faced was that everyone tended to do their own thing with no fear of negative consequences. It wasn't clear what behaviors would advance you in the company; and it seemed that no matter what you did, you couldn't be fired. It was the most open and permissive environment I'd ever been in, but with no defined rules or standards, there was almost no way to keep everyone rowing the boat in the same direction.

3. There is flexibility within the rules. Rather than serving as a straitjacket, they serve as a road map to allow staff to flourish. In the case Donald just described, new management was brought in, and a variety of new rules were put in place. The systems helped ensure consistency, but there were also ways to customize a solution when the rules didn't really fit too well.

4. People participate in the decision-making process. Change is the only constant in the home or workplace. We learned long ago that, when people feel they have a say in matters, they are much more likely to buy into decisions. When they don't, they are likely to rebel. Doris and Phil recall a particularly difficult transition in their business.

Doris and Phil

For twenty-four years in the travel business, we always paid our staff salaries based on skill and seniority. As the industry was changing, we realized that we had to move to a sales-driven, pay-for-performance (i.e., commission) system. We could have just announced this decision, but the consequences likely would have been severe. This big a change after so many years probably would have caused a great deal of fear—even to people whose sales were so strong that they would benefit from it.

Instead, we discussed the changes in the industry at a staff meeting without presenting any specific decisions about handling them. We asked for feedback and suggestions from the staff about ways the office could adapt to the new realities of the market. At the next meeting, we announced we were leaning toward a pay-for-performance system and discussed some general parameters. Again, we sought feedback and additional suggestions.

Finally, we announced the new plan. That same day, our office manager met with each and every employee to review what the change meant for them and what they could do to get the most out of it. Rather than reacting to this immense change in the naturally resistive way, the staff became comfortable with the new ideas. They knew they had a voice in it, and many now accepted that the new system would actually make them more money.

This was no different from the way we approached major family decisions when the kids were growing up! Democratic, or participatory, management worked the same in both situations.

5. People can learn from their mistakes. The desire to protect our children from harm is so great, it's easy to try to prevent bad things from happening. But deep down, we know that growth not only results from failure, it often requires it. With our office families, we want to provide the benefit of our wisdom and experience to save our employees from making mistakes. However, if we want them to grow, we have to give them room to experiment, to fail, and to learn from those mistakes. Back when Doug was managing a sales team, he encountered this situation.

Doug

My salesperson and I were meeting with a pretty important prospect. While we were reviewing the sales strategy, it was clear to me that my salesperson was making a fairly critical mistake. I asked why he was choosing this strategy. His response showed flawed logic, but he had a tremendous amount of conviction in it. At this point I had two choices: (a) correct the flaw and take over the strategy or (b) risk losing the sale. If I had corrected the strategy, it would have been me overruling the salesperson. He would have been upset and would have thought I was being bossy. We would get the sale, but we wouldn't improve the salesperson's capabilities. I did the only thing I could: I let him implement his strategy. What happened? We lost the sale.

Afterwards, we did a "sales autopsy." Through questioning, the salesperson realized the flaw, and as a result, he made better decisions in the future. He was much more open because he had thought he had a failsafe strategy and lost anyway. This was the necessary condition to prepare him to be willing to learn. The lost sale was a short-term defeat; the changes the salesperson now made were a big long-term win!

Natural and Logical Consequences

The principle of democratic leadership is best summed up by Dinkmeyer and McKay, who base a significant number of their leadership principles on the concept of "natural and logical consequences." This simply means that all of us, whether children in the home or employees at work, can make our own independent choices, but we must be prepared to live with the natural and logical consequences that will follow. Stay up late watching television rather than studying, and you must be prepared to fail the test. Stay up late and party every night rather than preparing for important meetings, and you must be prepared to watch others get promoted while you are not.

While designed to teach parents how to help children develop at home, the principles of natural and logical consequences as opposed to punishment apply equally to developing employees in the office.

1. Logical consequences express the reality of the social order, not of the person; punishment expresses the power of personal authority.

2. The logical consequence is logically related to the misbehavior; punishment only sometimes is.

3. Logical consequences imply no element of moral judgment; punishment often does.

4. Logical consequences are concerned only with what will happen now; punishment focuses on the past.

5. The voice is friendly when consequences are invoked; there is danger in punishment, either open or concealed.

Focusing on natural and logical consequences automatically implies we must accept employees for who they are. Dinkmeyer and McKay talk about how establishing a healthy atmosphere at home with children depends on accepting the child. *"This does not mean condoning all behavior. It's possible to disapprove of certain conduct without rejecting the child as a person."* They talk about how tone of voice and nonverbal communication must imply that the child is valued while the act is not.

"It's essential to separate the deed from the doer." This reminds us of an experience Doris and Phil had with one of the first teenagers they hired in a full-time job a number of years ago.

Doris and Phil

Natalie had excellent skills and worked well with clients when she was in a good mood (which was most of the time). However, she did not take criticism well and tended to respond in the tone of voice teenagers use with their parents when they are annoyed at being corrected. In addition, if we showed her a document she had created with a few errors, she would not see any problem or feel the need to take remedial action.

After a few incidents like this, we became somewhat impatient with Natalie's attitude. We didn't need a rebellious teenager's behavior in the business world. We also realized that, since a C is a completely acceptable grade in the minds of many students, she wasn't seeing that having "just a few errors" in a document was not acceptable. After all, it was at least C work. However, in the business world, there are usually only two grades available—A or F. Something is acceptable or it is not.

Since Natalie's capabilities and skills were excellent, we believed she had good potential and just needed to grow up. But we weren't going to give her a great amount of time to do so. We gave her a letter on a Friday afternoon, telling her she was on probation. In the letter, we indicated we knew she could do better, but she had to mature and get rid of that teenage attitude. We fully expected her to call in Monday and tell us that she wasn't returning.

We are happy to report that over the weekend she matured greatly. She came to work Monday with a completely different attitude. She had truly grown up over the weekend. She went on to become one of our best agents with a very helpful attitude and a willingness to learn from her errors and grow.

This is remarkably similar to Ken Blanchard's premise in *The One Minute Manager* when he discusses "one minute reprimands" (though by this point in the book, perhaps it's not so remarkable that many recognized parenting practices are the same as many recognized management practices). Blanchard emphasizes that reprimands that attack individuals and their worth are ultimately not productive. Rather, reprimands that clearly describe the undesirable behavior while emphasizing faith in the subordinate's natural ability to do better are ultimately motivating.

Donald

The day I was finishing up the first draft of this chapter, one of my colleagues and I were discussing various managers at work. On the one hand, we were criticizing one person who was known for constantly micromanaging and berating subordinates when things went wrong, whatever the cause. This manager was often successful with projects but burned through people and left a lot of dissatisfaction. People would eventually simply tune this manager out when reprimand time came yet again.

On the other hand, my colleague recalled another manager who had chewed his rear off—but only because he deserved it—yet emphasized his belief that my colleague could do better. It was years since it had happened, but he still remembered it and was self-motivated to never repeat that mistake and have that feeling again.

It made me think about my days with my parents when their disappointment in me (and mine in myself) was far more effective punishment than being shouted at.

Do we advocate that kids or employees be given choices about everything? Of course not. No more so than our democracy as a society has its citizens vote on every single issue. But we are saying that being a pushover is usually the wrong way to go, and overcompensating the other way doesn't help in the long run. Treat subordinates as "equal under the law" and let them have a say (but not the final say) in the direction of the office, and their work will lead to a healthier, happier, and, most importantly, more effective office.

Dr. Spock, who has been accused of advocating permissive child rearing only to then be accused of renouncing this philosophy and turning strict, sums it up perhaps best when he says, "If "permissive" means allowing children to have a say and do almost anything they want (which is what most people think it means), then I never had such a philosophy. Children themselves work hard to grow up, to be more mature, to become more responsible." He goes on to state that it is important, in all communications between parent and child, that parents demonstrate respect for themselves and ask their children to show respect for them as well.

We can't say it any better for managers (the office parents) and their employees (the office children) ourselves.

If you've never been hated by your child, you've never been a parent.
                                                                    —Bette Davis

Tips from Managers

1. Never intentionally "look the other way."

2. Watch out for situations where you are so caught up in your own work you miss signals from your subordinates.

3. It's not easy, but find the balance between professional distance and friendship with employees that best fits your personality.

4. Avoid an overly permissive, or "abdicratic," leadership style.

5. Set and enforce standards, but remember that strictness simply for strictness's sake rarely works well.

6. Create rules that have flexibility so you don't box yourself into a corner.

7. Create an environment of mutual respect.

8. Let subordinates participate in the decision process; this doesn't mean they have a vote, but they do have a voice.

9. Realize that sometimes failure is a better teacher than you are. You may be able to direct people away from failure, but they won't learn as much from the experience as they would by failing on their own.

10. Make people accountable for the "natural and logical" consequences of their actions rather than afraid of arbitrary punishments.

Tips from Employees

1. We may act really friendly, but we're not looking to our bosses for friends—we find friends among our peers or away from the office.

2. If we know you'll look the other way, we'll be happy to take advantage of you.

3. Recognize us for who we are—if we are unusually self-disciplined, then you can be more permissive.

4. You can force us, through strictness, to do things, but you won't win our hearts that way.

5. Trust us, and we are more likely to trust you.

6. We know you have to set rules, but make sure you allow enough flexibility for us to add our own personality and approach to our tasks.

7. Make sure you live by the same rules you require us to live by. We don't respect or react well to double standards.

8. Allow us to participate in the decision-making process, and we will be more likely to accept your decisions—even if we disagreed with them.

9. If you must punish us, make sure the punishment relates to the "crime."

10. We're not always going to like you, but that shouldn't be how you measure your success with us.

CHAPTER 10

Avoiding the Superparent Syndrome:
You Don't Have to Do Everything!

Today's women . . . have taken admirable giant strides forward politically, professionally, economically and educationally. Yet, when they become mothers, they indenture themselves to their children in perpetuity.

—John Rosemond
Honolulu Advertiser

Doris

Many times, after one of our seminars on personnel management, we have had one or more people come up to talk to us about how exhausted and frustrated they were and how their employees just weren't doing enough. One case I remember well is quite typical.

Betty had been the owner and manager of a moderate-size travel agency for several years. The office was open Monday, Tuesday, and Thursday from 9:00 A.M. to 5:00 P.M., Wednesday and Friday from 9:00 A.M. to 8:00 P.M., and Saturday from 2:00 P.M. to 4:00 P.M. However, although Betty found that her staff was usually able to get out of the office relatively on time, she was rarely able to leave before 9:00 or 10:00 any evening during the week.

Betty insisted that she couldn't afford to hire any more people and that there was just no way that she could get some of her own time and personal life back. She was exhausted and getting quite resentful of her staff, feeling that they were not offering to help but were just rushing out at the end of the official workday.

When we questioned Betty about her workload, she admitted that she handled all the VIP and longtime clients herself, as well as opening the mail every day and preparing the required weekly report of airline ticket sales. She also performed a variety of other clerical and maintenance tasks.

She complained that she didn't have the time to do any of the managerial functions we were suggesting since she couldn't complete her "normal" workload. When we suggested that she could turn over some of these tasks to other staff members, we received the same reply from her that we had heard many times from others with this complaint.

Betty insisted that she was the only one who could handle these very important clients and that she had to open the mail and do the report herself so that she would know what was happening beyond her own desk. We pointed out that she was not functioning as a manager at all, but rather as a senior salesperson since she was handling almost a full load of clients herself. We told her that her job as manager was to train others to do the work she had done in the past so she could get on to the functions she should be concentrating on.

We pointed out to her that the vast majority of the mail that was coming in every day was general, noncritical material and that she could teach someone how to handle those pieces and just give her the ones that she needed to see. We also told her that she didn't need to do the accounting reports herself, but that she should delegate that function to someone else and just look them over to know what was happening.

We hope that Betty took our advice when she returned to her office, but, unfortunately, we guess that she is like so many others who never really make the transition from frontline worker to manager. Instead, they continue to handle a full load of frontline functions themselves, while trying unsuccessfully to manage the office. These people are doomed to exhaustion since they are unwilling to train or trust their subordinates to take over important tasks or clients, and are also unwilling to let go of clerical tasks that a subordinate could easily perform.

If you've ever finished a chore that your child was supposed to do because it was easier to do it yourself than fight, then you've experienced the same frustration managers feel picking up the pieces of a project because it had not been done and the deadline is approaching. If you find yourself regularly working many hours after the office has closed trying to catch up on all the things on your "To Do" list, feel that there is just never enough time to do everything you have to do, or find yourself tired and edgy by the end of the day, then you have become a victim of what we call the ".Superparent Syndrome."

You are the last resort to make sure everything gets done, and your children or employees know they can count on you to do so. They don't really have to worry about finishing their assigned tasks on time because they know Mom or Dad will come to the rescue. They also know that, like most people, you will avoid confrontation even if such avoidance puts a greater burden on yourself. Worse yet, the more you do this, the more you train them to expect it, and the more you resign yourself to a life of indenture to people who are supposed to be helping you.

John Rosemond's column in the *Honolulu Advertiser* of June 12, 2000, which we quoted at the start of this chapter, goes on to make some other very excellent observations.

> The problem is that today's mothers are trying to clear what I term the "mother bar"—a contemporary standard of good mothering. It consists of messages to the effect that the best mother is the busiest mother, the most attentive mother, the mother who provides the most for her children, fixes it whenever they get upset, drops what she's doing at their beck and call, helps them nightly with their homework and makes sure each module of their brains is properly stimulated from the womb on.

> Contrast all of this with the typical mother of 50 years ago. That very formidable woman intimidated her children. They did not intimidate her. She was not their servant, but rather there to teach them to stand on their own two feet.

This could just as easily have been written about many of today's managers. Although the article speaks specifically about women, it is true of many men as well.

What Is a Manager?

Management is often defined as "getting work accomplished through others." This requires delegating activities to staff members and then allowing them to do the work that has been assigned. Good managers get more ego satisfaction from seeing subordinates successfully complete new tasks than from doing such things themselves. As long as you have to "do it yourself" to get it done right, there will never be enough time for everything you have to do and many of the managerial tasks will be left undone. And many tasks that could have been assigned to others will dominate your time, energy, and talents.

There is a well-known story (author is unknown) that demonstrates a typical scenario in most homes and offices.

> This is a story about four people named Everybody, Somebody, Anybody, and Nobody. There was an important job to be done and Everybody was sure that Somebody would do it. Anybody could have done it, but Nobody did it. Somebody got angry about that because it was Everybody's job. Everybody thought Anybody could do it, but Nobody realized that Everybody wouldn't do it. It ended up that Everybody blamed Somebody when Nobody did what Anybody could have done!

This scenario is the result of poor management. No job should be "everybody's" responsibility. That makes it nobody's responsibility. Within an office, every task should be assigned to a specific person, perhaps with a backup person in the event of the absence of the primary person. Only then will everyone understand who is responsible when a job is left undone. For repetitive maintenance tasks, responsibility can be rotated so no one person always has to do the "grunge" work, but everyone should know just who is responsible at any given time for any given task.

Delegating effectively is a learned skill and one that all managers should learn in their early days of managing. Without developing delegation skills, a manager will never have enough time, and employees will feel distrusted and abused.

Donald

I remember as a child constantly striving to be given more responsibility, to prove I was able to do things on my own. Now, with two girls of my own, I see the same from them. When my daughter Erika was about five, nothing made her happier than being able to declare, "I did it myself," and nothing was more insulting to her than trying to do something for her she knew she could do. There was no rebuke more stinging from her than "I can do that myself, Daddy!" I saw the same behavior in Daria, my younger daughter, when she was about one and could not even talk. She saw Erika doing something, and she wanted to do it, too.

Not surprisingly, the same is true with adults. At work, I often mentor younger, less experienced consultants and managers. Their reaction to the first time they master a complex task comes in a close second to the pride I've seen in Erika.

Anyone can learn to delegate, but they must first be willing to let go of tasks they are used to handling and allow someone else to take over. The important thing here is, don't let your ego of "it takes me to get the job done" get in the way of getting the job done. Managers who can't get over the fear of letting employees do something on their own because they might screw up are no different from parents who are unwilling to teach their children to set the table or wash the dishes because the children might break something.

Doris

When we promoted our assistant manager, Jeanette, to manager several years ago, she was our top salesperson and was used to being proud of how well she handled clients. She would get very frustrated when a subordinate did not sell as effectively or used a different technique, even when it was successful.

Since Jeanette certainly was capable of becoming an excellent manager, we worked with her for a few months and even had her attend one of our personnel-management seminars. One of the concepts we stressed, since most of the managers in the seminar were really functioning as the top salesperson in their office instead of as managers, was that a manager had to receive ego satisfaction from what subordinates did and from how well the manager had taught them, rather than from their own production.

"Show us an office where the manager is the top performer," we always said, "and we'll show you an office that isn't being managed."

One day, a couple of weeks after the seminar, Jeanette came to me very proudly and told me that she now understood what we had meant in the seminar. She was extremely proud of how one of our employees had worked with a client since it was based on what Jeanette had just taught her. She stated that she now really felt like a manager and understood the difference.

Doug, however, had a different experience while he was still in college.

Doug

One summer during college, I worked as a floor salesman at a discount appliance store. I quickly became the top salesperson at the store. Instead of enjoying my success and feeling that he was partially responsible for it, the manager began to get jealous of my sales volume. I noticed that, as soon as I started to offer help to a likely prospect, he would frequently intervene and take over the sale so he would get the credit for it. It was obvious that he felt there was a competition between us and that, as the manager, he would lose face if his sales didn't top mine. Needless to say, I didn't work there very long, since I had no desire to be in competition with my manager. This experience taught me that a manager must be support-ive of the efforts of subordinates and take pleasure from their successes. There should never be a competition between the parent and the child.

There is no question—it takes more time to teach someone else to do something than to do it yourself. This is another excuse used when managers haven't taught others to perform tasks previously handled personally. We hear statements like, "I'd love to teach someone else to do this, but I'm always so busy that I just don't have the time to teach anyone." If you have this atti-tude, the one thing we can guarantee is that you'll never get the time. You will always be a slave to the rest of the family, who gets to go home on time.

It takes time to teach someone. If the task is a onetime thing that will never come up again, or that might only be done once a year, doing it yourself is often valid since you won't save any time. However, for repet-itive tasks, the time you invest in teaching people will pay off. The first time you are teaching the task, it will take more time than doing it your-self. The second time, while you are supervising the task being done by the person to whom you've delegated it, it should take about the same as

"Wouldn't it be easier to learn how to delegate authority, Bob?"

doing it yourself. But, after that, you will save time every single time the task is done and you don't need to be there. The cumulative savings are enormous, especially when you multiply the time saved by the number of tasks that can be delegated.

One of our favorite sayings when teaching managers to delegate more effectively is "Give a person a fish, and you've given them a meal. Teach a person to fish, and you've given them a livelihood."

Steps to Delegating Effectively

Choose the delegatee carefully. Delegate to someone with skills appropriate to learning this task or who is "right" for handling this customer. Do not just delegate to the first person who passes by your desk when you decide to delegate. Try to match the task to the best person capable of handling it.

Let employees know that you feel that they are now ready to grow to this level and to take over tasks or situations that you have handled yourself in the past. Let them know that you respect their abilities and trust them with these new functions. Don't give the impression that you are just trying to get rid of tasks or clients you don't want.

Remember that, at first, they will probably not be able to perform the job as well or as quickly as you have been doing. You weren't so good or so fast when you first started either. Give them the time to get used to new tasks—they will improve in both quality and speed over time. Don't be tempted to take back a job to get it done faster or "better." Remember, you are seeking to save time in the long term, not the short term.

Be sure to delegate a reasonable amount of work and responsibility at first. Don't overload someone with too much at once. Give them a task in pieces if it is a complex one. That way they can learn more easily and more thoroughly and not become intimidated by being responsible for too much too soon. As they get more experienced, add to their responsibility appropriately.

Do not demand that others perform tasks exactly as you would have. Merely judge if the final results are adequate for what is needed. Give your staff space to put their own marks on the functions. You may be surprised—they may come up with something even better than you did. If this happens, you should be proud of what they have done, not jealous or threatened. Parents who expect their kids to behave as their clones, doing everything exactly as they would, are rarely successful. Parents who take pride in watching their children put their own stamp on how they do things, and celebrate when their children's ability at times exceeds their own, are usually successful.

When delegating, make sure your instructions are clear and understood. If there is any complexity, you might want to put the instructions in writing so the assigned employee can check what they are doing as they proceed.

Make sure that employees know when jobs should be finished and, if they are lengthy, periodically check progress at agreed-upon points. Remember, however, you are merely checking and asking if help is needed—you are not going to take over the tasks.

When weaning important customers from you to a subordinate, you may need to do it gradually so the client doesn't get nervous. You might talk to the client when they call and ask for you, but have your subordinate do the research and get back to the client. Your subordinate can tell the client that you had asked them to call back since you had to leave the office and you didn't want to keep the customer waiting. If you have delegated the customer to a person who is right for that customer, after several such interactions, you will find the customer calling your subordinate directly and hardly realizing that they have been weaned from you. You must guard against resenting that the client is now quite happy with your subordinate. If you need to be indispensable, you will never get out from under your

*"Reversing the earth's rotation **would** give us an extra month, Stacey. But we decided to delegate the project instead."*

load. Enjoy the freedom that delegation has provided.

There is another type of delegation that has crippled many managers. It's called "upward delegation," situations where subordinates delegate tasks up to you that they can handle themselves. Many parents and managers fall prey to upward delegation.

Phil

Maria was a dedicated manager at a company we consulted with who did her best to help train and motivate her employees. However, like many parents, she was sometimes too ready to do things for them that they could do for themselves. As with many others we've helped, she was in the position of not having the time for her own work.

After visiting her office and observing for a little while, we saw one of the major problems. Consistently, one or another of her employees would approach Maria and request that she take care of some difficulty they were having. They brought a variety of problems, things like a complaint from a customer, a challenge with a vendor, and the need to write a letter to explain something to a customer. Maria would tell her employees to leave them on her desk, and she would take care of them.

Maria was letting her subordinates free up their time and ease their burden by delegating tasks to her; hence the term, "upward delegation." At least subconsciously, employees call it "getting the monkey off my back." When managers accept responsibility for taking care of their employees' problems, they are adding monkeys to their own backs. Often, the weight becomes crushing.

Maria had her own list of things she needed to do that day, but the list of things her staff had handed over to her, with her permission, was growing. In addition to getting more things on her desk that she now had taken responsibility for, Maria was teaching her employees to just turn them over to her.

This is very much like what happened to the mother described in the *Honolulu Advertiser* column earlier in this chapter. Maria was trying very hard to make life easy for her employees and, in doing so, was preventing them from learning how to take care of their own problems. Ken Blanchard, in his book *The One Minute Manager Meets the Monkey,* talks about letting everyone in the office get rid of the monkeys on their backs by putting them on the manager's back.

Now, in Maria's case, if each of her five employees gave her just one new monkey each day, she would gain five new monkeys to handle in addition to the two or three monkeys of her own that she already had.

Each employee has lost the pressure of one monkey and Maria now has seven or eight. No wonder she never had time for her own work.

There is a simple way to avoid upward delegation. Make sure that, unless something absolutely and truly must have the specific attention of the manager, an employee who comes into the manager's office with a monkey should leave with the same monkey still on his or her back, but with some advice on handling the situation. Maria should have advised each employee what to say to the customer, whom to call to get satisfaction from the vendor, and how to write the letter. This way the employees would learn how to handle similar situations in the future and would no longer need to bring them to Maria's attention.

Helping employees is an important aspect of management. However, managers have two other responsibilities that may conflict with their instinct to be helpful. The first is to help employees develop and become self-sufficient and productive. The second responsibility is to themselves—to perform their other management functions and (even if they don't believe it) to have a life outside the office.

Instead of just advising an employee of how to take care of the problem, Maria should have asked each employee what they thought should be done. In many cases, they already know what should be done, but are just insecure about doing it. This is just like Mom or Dad, when Junior asks how to spell a word, responding: "How do you think it's spelled?" It is better to see if they have an idea and to help them think it through than to just supply the answer—we're back to the fish analogy. However, if they are completely lost on what to do, then a parent who wants to help a child learn will walk them through the thought process and help them get to the answer. This technique might even take more time than taking care of the problem yourself, but the employee will have learned an additional skill that will save everyone time whenever a similar situation arises.

Doris

When I was a child and wanted to know what a word meant, my father always made me look it up in the dictionary myself. It drove me nuts, but it taught me to be more self-sufficient. In the office, I try to direct employees to the appropriate resource themselves rather than simply provide the answer. It may annoy them, but they and I are proud of how self-sufficient they become.

Another challenge many managers face is the temptation to come in and rescue an employee who has not completed an assigned task by the deadline. Too many managers, upon finding out an hour before the deadline that a job is not finished yet, jump right in and take it over, relieving the employee of the necessity of finishing it. Even if employees "get in trouble" for this type of failure, they learn that they can get away with not finishing things they don't enjoy doing because their manager will come to their rescue. Then, the managers wonder why this happens over and over again.

Some employees, just like many children, would rather put up with the lecture or other punishment than with finishing a chore they don't want to do. It is critical that employees finish their projects even if the manager has to check back every few minutes to make sure they do so. This teaches them to finish such tasks before the manager finds out something isn't done.

Managers also need to learn to "tune out" the normal sounds and distractions of the office, yet keep their antennae up for the unusual that might require intervention. Remember, however, that an intervention does not automatically mean taking the challenge over and doing it—it merely means discovering the challenges before they become crises and helping someone else do whatever needs to be done.

Once parents and managers learn to delegate, they free up great amounts of time to focus on the tasks that properly lay within their realm. However, there is one more skill they need. That is the ability to manage their time effectively.

Managing Your Time

Time management, like delegation, is a learned skill. There are basic steps that people can take to maximize their use of time. There's an old story about Ben Franklin that shows his appreciation of the value of time.

One day Ben Franklin was busy preparing his newspaper for printing when a customer stopped in his store and spent an hour browsing through various books for sale. Finally, he took one in his hand and asked the shop assistant the cost.

The assistant answered: "One dollar."

The customer said: "A dollar. Can't you sell it for less?"

The assistant said: "No. The price is a dollar."

The customer said he wanted to see Mr. Franklin. When Franklin appeared from the back room, the customer asked how much he wanted for the book.

Franklin said: "One dollar and a quarter."

The customer was taken aback. "Your assistant only asked for a dollar."

Franklin said: "If you had bought it from him, I could sell it to you for a dollar. But you have taken me away from the business I was engaged in."

The customer pressed on. "Come on, Mr. Franklin, what is the lowest you can take for it?"

Franklin said: "One dollar and a half. And the longer we take to discuss it, the more I'll have to charge you."

There is no doubt that Ben Franklin understood the value of time. Unfortunately, most people do not. Time is our most valuable resource. We all have the same amount available, but there are vast differences in how we use this precious commodity.

Do you fit the profile of many busy managers we have met? You are always busy, but never seem to complete your important work. Your office closes at 5:00 P.M., but you usually must keep working until 8:00 P.M. Many of us fall into this pattern, but we must break out of it before we are burned out.

Jack Welch, chairman and CEO of General Electric and one of the most celebrated CEOs of his time, has said on many occasions that, regardless of your job, if it takes more than forty hours a week to do your job you're doing something wrong.

Ben Franklin said it best more than two hundred years ago: "The supply of time is a daily miracle; you wake up with it in the morning and your wallet is magically filled. No one receives more or less than you do." No amount of money or intelligence can give anyone more time. People can, however, choose to use their time differently.

We all set priorities, whether or not we realize it. Some of us invest a small amount of time up front to set our priorities in a conscious, businesslike manner. Effective time management requires logical, conscious setting of priorities.

Time management has become an industry in itself. Many books have been written on the subject and many manual and electronic items are available to assist busy people with controlling their activities.

One of the biggest problems with time management systems is that many users become slaves to their systems and forget why they are using them. Time is wasted on playing with systems, at the expense of actually working on priorities.

It is not necessary to spend a lot of money on systems to set proper priorities. A simple "To Do" list works very effectively. Update your list daily, either at the end of the day in preparation for tomorrow or at the beginning of your day (before leaving home or immediately upon getting to your office). However, make sure that you have prepared a written To Do list, not a set of little pieces of paper that can misplaced or a list that is only in your mind. If it is not written down, it doesn't exist.

Prioritize items into A, B, and C categories. The A level is for projects that are important and need to be done very soon. B items are important but not quite as urgent. C items are those tasks you would like to get to when you have the time. For jobs that do not need to be done within the next few days, keep a "tickler" file where you enter the task and a date a few days prior to its deadline. That way, you will remember to include the task in your To Do list at the appropriate time.

With a To Do list organized in this manner, you can be sure that you work on A items before getting to the B priorities and that you don't waste time on those C items unless all A and B items are under control. Without categorizing a To Do list in this manner, there is a tendency to complete lots of small, unimportant C tasks just so we can feel good checking items off our list, even though none of the things we have accomplished in the last hour were really important, and we are still looking at a major, critical task that we have been avoiding. Many of the C items may never get done, but they are items that do not *have* to be finished.

If you are afraid of being buried in lists, there is an even easier technique some people use effectively. Each day, when you get to the office, write down the three most important tasks to be performed that day—and do them!

With a continuing To Do list, you will never have to worry about forgetting a job. It is right there on your list. Most people spend so much time thinking about all the other things they have to do and are afraid they will forget that they cannot concentrate on the task at hand. With a To Do list, you can concentrate on what you are doing, put everything else out of your mind, and work much more efficiently. Your memory is not in your head—it is on your list.

If you'd like to learn more about how to set up effective life and time management systems for yourself, the most useful program we've come across is put out by Franklin Covey. You can find out more about their programs at www.franklincovey.com.

One other little "trick" is to keep a list of quick chores that you can accomplish while on hold on the telephone. Hold time can add up to hours over time. Examples of such quick chores include cleaning up old files on the computer, writing short memos, going through your mail, reading trade publications, etc. Such use of this otherwise "down" time will save you valuable time elsewhere.

There are a number of other techniques that can help managers maximize their use of time. Ask yourself the following questions:

What am I thinking about at this moment? If your mind is wandering and you are not thinking about the task you are involved in, you are not going to be as effective as you could be. If you are "not in the mood" for a particular job, you will prolong the agony. Push yourself to get that job done so that you can get to the next, hopefully more enjoyable job. Concentrate only on the specific task of the moment and put everything else out of your mind.

Do I say yes too often? In sorting out demands on your time, learn when to say no. It is good to help others, but be sure you are not assisting so much that you don't have enough time in the normal working day to get to your own category A tasks. Be wary of those times when your staff is trying to delegate upwardly to you.

Do I give myself the time to do things I want to do? If you are regularly staying late at the office, you need to restructure your priorities. Create an A level priority of giving yourself some time that is really yours. Busy managers need to have their To Do list cover both their business and personal needs. Otherwise, their business life will take over their personal life. Doris, for example, has made it a policy for several years to avoid working on any business-related tasks on Friday evenings. Even being a couch potato is a meaningful activity if it lets you relax and refresh yourself once a week. Doug has a policy of "free days" when he will not discuss or conduct any business activity, but instead he can concentrate on his family, read a book, or just unwind. Even workaholics who love their work need to take some timeouts to recharge their energies. Obviously, a dire emergency will take precedence, but be sure it is something that really can't wait before giving up your planned free time.

Parents, whether at home or in the office, all have the same complaint—there's never enough time to do all the things they want to do. We need to accept the fact that there never will be. Therefore, we have to choose just how to most effectively spend the limited time we have. When we continuously overextend ourselves, we become just like the exhausted mother who snaps back and overreacts at the slightest request from one of her children.

Above all, be flexible in managing time effectively. Don't over-organize. Don't waste time worrying about tomorrow. If in doubt about how you are spending your allotted amount of time, ask yourself the following question from Alan Lakein, a noted time management specialist: "What is the best use of my time—right now?"

> Time management is an invaluable skill, and I honed mine running a household and a business simultaneously. Once you've dressed a struggling infant in a snowsuit, argued about the gas bill and composed an enticing ad—all while the meatloaf bakes in the oven—the rest is a breeze.
>
> —Lillian Vernon
> *An Eye for Winners*

Tips from Managers

1. Do not feel that you have to take over every problem that an employee encounters. Help them learn how to handle it themselves.

2. Do not allow upward delegation unless it is something that really, really needs your contacts or abilities. Help employees decide on the next step and let them do it.

3. Train your employees to take over some of your functions and then trust them to do so.

4. Make sure that all necessary tasks for your office are assigned to a specific person so that there can be accountability when something is not done on time.

5. Learn to satisfy your ego by seeing your subordinates succeed, and take pride when they can do something even better than you can.

6. Remember Ben Franklin's example. Don't allow other people to "waste" your time.

7. Set your priorities and maintain a daily written To Do list that is categorized by urgency.

8. When you are working on a task, dedicate your full attention to that task and that task only. If you cannot avoid getting distracted, then take care of whatever is distracting you before going back to the original job.

9. Don't waste time worrying about things. If you can control what is worrying you, then do so. If it is not within your control, then get it out of your mind until you can do something about it.

10. Plan time for yourself in both your business and private life. In fact, make sure to maintain a private life outside of the business.

Tips from Employees

1. Please delegate tasks to me when I feel I am ready to handle them and encourage me to be ready for new challenges.

2. When you delegate a job to me, please trust me to finish it. I will come to you if I have a problem. It is all right to check up on how I'm coming along, but please make it apparent that you have put your trust in me to do the job.

3. If I try to hand a problem over to you that you think I should be able to handle myself, gently remind me about my own abilities rather than getting annoyed with me.

4. On the other hand, when I come to you with a challenge, please don't take it over yourself as if you do not trust me to handle it. I usually just want some advice to make sure I am heading in the right direction. I want to finish it myself.

5. When I have done a good job with an assignment, please feel free to praise my work. It makes me feel good and I will work even harder on the next task.

6. If I appear to be caught up and others in the office need help, please let me know how I can assist them.

7. If you delegate a task to me, let me know when it is due and how urgent that deadline is so that I can set the proper priorities on my work.

8. Please make it clear to all of us who is responsible for what so that we don't become victims of the Everybody, Somebody, Anybody, Nobody scenario.

9. Remember that I do have an important life outside the office. I will try to help out as much as possible, but sometimes I cannot stay late or come in on a weekend because of personal commitments.

10. Realize that we do not think more of you because you stay late every night. We are more comfortable if you are organized and can delegate effectively so that you, too, can leave the office on time most of the time.

CHAPTER 11

You Can't Be Perfect:
So Why Try?

The day the child realizes that all adults are imperfect he becomes an adolescent; the day he forgives them, he becomes an adult; the day he forgives
himself he becomes wise. —Alden Nowlan
Between Tears and Laughter

Doris
*Once, when Donald was a junior in high school, I asked him why,
although he was receiving As with grades on tests or projects usually in
the 90-91 percent range, he never chose to do any "extra credit" work
teachers assigned. I felt that he should sometimes do that extra work just
for his own satisfaction.*

*Donald looked at me and asked me why he should do the extra work.
He pointed out that he wouldn't really learn anything more than he was
already learning, and he was going to get As on his report card anyway.
He also pointed out that the additional time it would take to bring his
average up from his typical 91 percent would take away from the time he
had for soccer, his school's "It's Academic" team, and just plain relaxing,
without any tangible advantage to him. He told me, long before he ever
worked in the business world, that "from a cost-benefits perspective," it
would be a waste of his time. Although I wanted him to do more, I had to
agree with his logic.*

*Donald went on to become the valedictorian of his graduation class. He
rarely had perfect scores, and he was seldom the highest-ranking student*

*in any individual class. He even had a knack for knowing which teachers
would round an 89.5 percent up to an A and which wouldn't. However, with
his "barely earned" As in all his subjects, he performed exactly as he needed to earn top honors.*

Donald, even as a teenager, mastered something many parents and
managers have yet to master—understanding the difference between perfection and "good enough." He had an excellent ability to set goals and
do the work necessary to meet them. He would not settle for inferior
work, but he also understood that sometimes a thing is good enough for
meeting the goal, and any extra time and effort spent to make it still better is really wasted. The time would be better spent on other endeavors.
He knew that the enemy of good is the best.

Focusing too much on perfection often distracts attention from what is
really important, as parenting and managing experts often caution.
Donald pursued "good enough" rather than "perfection" because he realized he could accomplish more by keeping his standards aligned with
those set by his teachers. At the opposite extreme, we've seen people so
focused on their own artificial standards of "perfection" that they risk
never achieving any meaningful goals.

Doris

*For more than ten years, Phil and I ran a study group to help people
within the travel industry become Certified Travel Counselors (CTC). The
CTC designation is the highest independent certification in this profes-
sion and is earned through graduate-level classes and tests, kind of like a
CPA of the travel industry. Over the years, several hundred people came
through our study groups. In order to gain the certification, they also had
to finish an additional project, which usually involved writing a "term
paper" on an approved subject.*

*One of the participants in our original group, Judy, had easily com-
pleted the testing part of the curriculum but had become stuck on that last
part. Judy was a perfectionist. She was writing her paper on traveling
with pets, and no matter how many drafts she wrote, she was never satisfied that it was "good enough." So she never turned it in, and she never
received her certification!*

*When we had been running the study group for ten years, we decided to
hold a reunion for the agents whom we had helped earn their certifications.
We wanted to honor the participants from the original group, who had been
the pioneers that set the tone for all who followed. Judy was the only living*

*alumna of the original group who had not received certification. We called
her and found out that she had written the required paper years ago but
wasn't satisfied enough to submit it. I talked her into sending me a copy.
The paper was fine. I begged her to send it in—saying that her goal was not
to submit the "perfect" paper but merely one that was good enough to meet
the requirements. I laid some guilt on her that she was the only barrier to
our original group's 100 percent record of certification.*

*She sent the paper in and, at the function, joined the rest of us from the
original group.*

As any parenting expert will tell you, there is a difference between perfect, which can never be achieved, and good, or even excellent, which can. Judy was afraid of anything less than perfection and, therefore, her paper could never satisfy her. When we convinced her to be satisfied with good, she got her certification.

The perfection syndrome plays out in parenting in two different ways:

1. The feeling that we, as parents, must be perfect. This manifests itself in the mistaken belief that any sign of being wrong will be perceived by children as a weakness that will undermine our credibility when it counts.

2. An inability to tolerate imperfection in our children. This manifests itself in many ways, from the parents who push kids in athletics to those who will bear no breach of however they perceive their children should behave.

The Perfect Parent—No Such Thing

We all want to be perfect parents at home and perfect managers at the office. It's as natural as Boston Red Sox fans wanting their team to win the World Series—and almost equally unlikely!

We all know we can't be perfect. Some of us accept this and make the most of what we have, yet others can't help but suffer the irony of *increasing their imperfection* by trying too hard to be perfect. Dr. Thomas Gordon so eloquently describes this phenomenon among parents in his book, *P. E. T. Parent Effectiveness Training.* Substitute "manager" for "parent," and the same quote describes what we've seen in so many cases during our many years of managing and consulting for other managers.

When parents become parents, something strange and unfortunate happens. They begin to assume a role or act a part and forget that they are persons. . . . In a very serious way, this transformation is unfortunate, because it so often results in parents forgetting they are still humans with human faults, persons with personal limitations, real people with real feelings. . . .

This terrible burden of responsibility brings a challenge to these persons-turned-parents. They feel they must always be consistent in their feelings, must always be loving of their children, must be unconditionally accepting and tolerant, must put aside their own selfish needs and sacrifice for the children, must be fair at all times, and above all must not make the mistakes their own parents made with them. . . .

Forgetting one's human-ness is the first serious mistake one can make on entering parenthood. An effective parent lets himself be a person—a real person. Children deeply appreciate this quality of realness and humanness in their parents.

Parents and managers who think that they are supposed to be perfect rarely succeed. If you rarely admit you are wrong, often look for other places or people on which to lay the blame, or often worry about letting your subordinates take chances, then you're in this group of overprotective wannabe-perfect managers. Unfortunately, just as children of overly protective parents learn at a very early age to be afraid of being wrong, so too will your subordinates learn quickly to be afraid of you.

Fear not, though. Your own behavior may be scripted by your fears, but it can be controllable. Children subordinate to overprotective adults learn quickly that Mom or Dad gets mad when they do something they're not supposed to do, that red marks on their tests are bad, that coaches don't like it when they make a mistake in sports, etc. It's no surprise, then, that many children take the fear of being wrong into adulthood—into their work life, and ultimately into their management style.

Control your worrying and demonstrate your own willingness to be "imperfect," and it's amazing the improvement you'll see. Note that we don't say "ignore" your worrying. That's impossible. You will worry, and taking new chances will probably scare the heck out of you. But every time you feel worry, do something consciously to turn the negative energy of worry into some positive action. You may start by remembering a saying that Doris's mother always used that we only found out years later is known as the Serenity Prayer and is one of the foundations of Alcoholics Anonymous and other addiction-oriented support groups. It is something we should all remember when we are worrying about making things perfect.

God, grant me the serenity
To accept the things I cannot change,
The courage to change the things I can,
And the wisdom to know the difference.

When we are too worried about perfection, we discourage our employees and ourselves from taking chances. If they never try anything new, they won't make mistakes. If you take no risks, it's hard to fail. They also won't learn new things or grow and the business will never be a leader in innovation. If your own drive for perfection makes it clear that failure will not be tolerated, then avoiding making a mistake is a stronger motivator than the possibility of doing well.

If we fail at a major undertaking, such as a new marketing venture, we should conduct a full debriefing, involving our entire team so we can try to determine what went wrong. Was it just a bad idea or did we execute it poorly? Do we want to try again with some adjustments?

Donald

When I first came into my parents' travel agency, we had decided to focus on selling cruises and become less dependent on airline tickets. I wanted to run a "cruise night," but my mother was somewhat gun-shy since they had tried to run one a few years earlier that had been a complete failure. We sat down together and analyzed what we felt had gone wrong.

We finally came to the conclusion that we had tried to run it at the wrong time of year for our community and that we had been afraid to spend enough money promoting it to make it successful. We were so afraid of losing money that we doomed the event to failure.

We decided, with much hesitation on my mother's part, to go ahead and do it "right." We chose a better time of year, rented a place instead of saving money by trying to hold it in our own office, and spent several thousand dollars on promotion. At the first cruise night, more than three hundred people attended and we sold more than enough cruises to provide a substantial profit over the event's costs. Although I am no longer working in my parents' agency, they have run ten of these and it has become their most successful annual event.

If Mom had continued to be afraid because of the agency's single failed attempt, we would never have had the annual successes we have enjoyed since. Perhaps more importantly, I would have been discouraged from taking chances—some of which have definitely failed, but many more of which have succeeded.

We have tried to teach managers of businesses that if they have never failed at any marketing venture, then they haven't tried enough. This, of course, does not mean that you just go out and try any idea that comes into your head. Good managers analyze the potential success of any new venture being considered. Successful managers, however, do not require guarantees of success—just good probability.

Successful companies must forge new paths or they will always be behind their competitors. Success requires at least occasional failure. There is a famous story about Thomas Edison, who was asked after countless failures on his way to inventing the electric bulb how he was able to stay motivated. He replied that he had no failures. He merely successfully found a number of ways that wouldn't work. This is the attitude of a successful, creative person, and it must be encouraged in subordinates if a business is really going to do well.

Mistakes or failures are not end results. They are merely barriers on the way to success. When we make a mistake, we should not waste time getting emotional or worrying about it. We should correct the problem as well as we can and move on. We should analyze why it went wrong so we can avoid making the same mistake in the future. Making a mistake is not a tragedy—making the same mistake over and over is.

Babe Ruth and Wayne Gretzky have both been immensely famous and popular in their respective sports of baseball and hockey. Babe Ruth is best known as the homerun king and Wayne Gretzky for scoring the most goals. What people forget is that Ruth was also the strikeout king. Without going through all those strikeouts, he would not have hit all those homeruns. Gretzky also holds the record for shots on goal, the majority of which did not result in goals. But without those "failed" shots, he could not have made the number of goals he made. As he once said, "You never make the shot you didn't take."

Parents and managers don't have to be all-knowing, expert at everything, and never wrong. They need to be real people with all the faults that human beings have. However, they need to show courage to make decisions and take a stand when necessary. They need leadership skills so their children or employees will not be afraid of the world around them.

This fear of losing respect if we are found wrong is misplaced. In actuality, people who admit their errors and take responsibility are respected more than those who don't. Sometimes, even old clichés still ring true. When it comes to leadership, honesty is truly the best policy. According to surveys of more than 7,500 managers in both public and private sectors, honesty was the trait most often mentioned by employees when describing a good leader.

Another survey of 15,000 people asked which of twenty traits were most important for someone in a leadership position. The top trait, by far,

"We prefer our leadership skills to be a little more subtle, Dale."

was being honest. The next three were being forward-looking, being inspirational, and being competent. Admitting to mistakes, as long as mistakes are not the norm, will be more than overcome by honesty to gain subordinates' respect and trust. Honest people, according to James M. Kouzes and Barry Z. Posner in their book, *Credibility: How Leaders Gain and Lose It, Why People Demand It,* have credibility.

Other characteristics that were admired in leaders were:

1. They keep promises. They do what they say they will do.

2. Their actions are consistent with the desires of the people they lead. They understand the values of their subordinates.

3. They believe in the value of other people.

4. They admit their mistakes.

5. They generate optimistic feelings in others and help their people feel good about their potential success.

6. They create a climate for learning through openness and trust.

This should send a message to all managers. Be open and forthright in your dealings with your employees. Respect from subordinates is an important part of leadership. Respect must be earned; it does not come automatically. Honesty breeds respect.

The Perfect Child—Don't Even Think About It

Kids will be kids, and employees will be employees. It's trite but true. So why do parents and managers pretend anything else? Parenting experts regularly comment that a parent's job is more about preparing their children for the challenges they'll face in life and how to deal with the inevitable failures that will come along than it is about ensuring they never fail. Managers, too, should focus more on how to help employees turn failures into positive experiences—or at least minimize the damage.

When mistakes are made, people use several techniques to dodge responsibility. One technique is avoidance—hoping that no one will notice. Frequently, this turns a minor error that could easily have been corrected into a major crisis that must be brought to someone's attention.

Phil

In our own agency in our early years, we had a relatively new employee, Joannie, who made a mistake. She had made a reservation for a client for travel over an upcoming holiday period. She had booked the airline flights and issued the ticket for the client. However, a few days later when she brought the record up to check something, she accidentally cancelled the reservation and was not able to get the seats back.

Hoping that she would be able to get the space back by herself, without anyone knowing about her error, Joannie kept checking the airline every few days to see if space cleared. When, three days before the planned departure, she had still not been able to find space anywhere near the price she had originally booked, she fearfully came to our manager to admit her error.

Had Joannie told the manager about the problem the day she discovered it, we could have solved it with one phone call to a high-level contact at that airline. However, after waiting almost two months, there was no way to get back what we originally had booked and ticketed. We were forced to pay for a much higher priced ticket on a slightly different itinerary to meet our commitment to our customer.

What we learned from this experience was that, even if we were very tolerant and understanding of an employee's honest mistake, we needed to make sure our employees truly understood our tolerance. As we mentioned earlier, employees come to us with their own deep-seated fears of punishment or rejection developed from how their own parents had treated mistakes. We must assure them that, as long as a mistake was an honest one, we will work with them. This does not mean, however, that they can make countless mistakes without any penalty. It means that as long as they have tried to do a good job, we understand that sometimes errors will be made along the way.

Creating an atmosphere of trust in an office is one of the most important and effective things a manager can do. When employees know they can speak honestly about a mistake without undue fear, we know we have created the right environment.

An unfortunate fact of life is that people will make mistakes—and these mistakes will cost time and money. How we react has a lot to do with the office atmosphere we create. If we immediately look for the opportunity to get angry and lay blame at somebody's feet, we create an atmosphere of distrust and fear. Employees will attempt to hide mistakes from us until they become too big to cover up. The result will be greater loss than if they had asked for advice or help earlier.

On the other hand, if we first focus on how to solve the problem, we let our employees know that they can trust us enough to make us aware of problems before they become too big to handle. While we cannot afford to allow employees to make the same mistakes repeatedly, we must allow them the opportunity to learn from their mistakes. Children will always remember the words they missed on the spelling test much more than the ones they accidentally got right.

Placing blame doesn't really accomplish much anyway. Employees know when they erred and often feel just as bad or worse than we do. The emotional energy that is wasted on seeking to lay blame can be put to much better use. In fact, we sometimes have to soothe one of our employees who is getting too upset about an error.

We need to search for creative solutions to minimize or eliminate the damage. After all, "we can't cry over spilled milk," but we can look for a way to clean it up and teach the person who spilled it how to hold the cup better in the future.

Another technique that people use to avoid responsibility for mistakes is denial. When an error is found, and there is no obvious one who is accountable, they stay silent or even deny that they committed it. A very popular theme used several times a year in the comic strip *Family Circus* shows something broken or some other mishap, with a little ghost in the room with the label Not Me on it. This is as frequent a happening in offices as it is in homes, with no one ever taking responsibility for a mishap and no one ever finding out who is responsible. It goes back to the Everybody, Somebody, Anybody, and Nobody story in the previous chapter.

The third reaction is to blame someone or something else. Even if they

admit the actual mistake, it is due to something other than their careless-
ness or lack of knowledge. There is an epidemic in our society of blam-
ing outside sources for our own mistakes. We find this in homes, offices,
and even in top levels of government.

The Secret to Success—"Flexible Consistency"

Since you can't be a perfect manager any more than you can be a perfect parent, what can you do? As managers, we've always liked the list of
"the three duties of a parent" presented by Sandra Hardin Gookin in
Parenting for Dummies: (1) being a positive role model, (2) being the
ever-present teacher, and (3) being the good friend.

Your employees look up to you as an example just as children look up
to their parents. As with parenting, you can either lead or be led—it's your
choice. You will make an impact, whether positive or negative, so why not
make it positive?

So many managers (and parents) worry about "doing things right."
They obsess about whether they're correct, and they fret over each time
they're wrong. But in our collective century of management experience,
we've found that leadership skills are more important to being a good role
model than management skills. What's the difference between leadership
and management? Perhaps no one has summarized this better than Warren
G. Bennis in his book *Leaders:* "Managers know how to do things right.
Leaders know how to do the right things." Bennis refers to the fact that
managers tend to make things happen according to plan, whether or not
the plan is the right thing to do. They make sure "the clock keeps ticking,"
even if it's telling the wrong time.

Phil

*I was once a staff vice-president for a trade association at the time a
new chief operating officer (COO) was appointed. This man was a manager who distrusted his staff and focused on petty matters at the expense
of important ones.*

*During his first week in the head position, he assigned one employee
to go around the office at 9:00 A.M. and take attendance of who was sitting at their desk and who was not. It did not matter what any person was
doing, how early they had come in to work, or how late they had worked
on previous days. All that mattered was that they were sitting at their desk
at 9:00 A.M. sharp.*

This focus on the form rather than the substance caused great dissatisfaction and low morale among many staff members. This man showed no interest in the overall mission of the association or appreciation of those employees who were contributing to the success of that mission. He merely focused on easily measurable traits such as where someone was at 9:00 A.M. In fact, he was so focused on such minutia that some employees who had arrived early and were working on a project away from their desk actually had to interrupt what they were doing to get back to their desk promptly at 9:00 A.M.

This manager was following the rules—everyone was supposed to be at work on time. He made sure they were doing things "right." Since he was a very poor leader and motivator, he forgot to see if they were doing the right things.

Needless to say, I left the organization within a few weeks after he became the COO.

Leaders, on the other hand, do the right thing—even if sometimes they're a bit disorganized about it. Being a good role model, like any aspect of leadership, doesn't mean that you have to be perfect. Leaders get upset, they make mistakes, and they sometimes misjudge things. More often than not, it's how they approach these mistakes that separates them from others. Do they wallow in their failures, or do they learn from them and move forward? When you encounter a challenge, do you curse the lemons you've been given, or do you make lemonade?

Gen. Colin Powell, in a presentation he calls "A Leadership Primer," gives sage advice:

> Perpetual optimism is a force multiplier. . . . Leaders who whine and blame engender those same behaviors among their colleagues. I am not talking about stoically accepting organizational stupidity and performance incompetence with a "what, me worry?" smile. I am talking about a gung-ho attitude that says, "We can change things here; we can achieve awesome goals; we can be the best." Spare me the grim litany of the "realist." Give me the unrealistic aspirations of the optimist any day.

Being a good role model/leader when it suits you isn't nearly enough. Just as children constantly take their cues from their parents, employees routinely observe their bosses and soak in what they see. That's why managers, like parents, must be ever-present teachers.

In another of General Powell's lessons, he gives more advice that is of equal use to parents and managers:

The day [subordinates] stop bringing you their problems is the day you have stopped leading them. They have either lost confidence that you can help them or concluded that you do not care. Either case is a failure of leadership. . . . Real leaders make themselves accessible and available. They show concern for the efforts and challenges faced by underlings, even as they demand high standards. Accordingly, they are more likely to create an environment where problem analysis replaces blame.

Stay close to the action. You need to be visible to your employees. Practice MBWA (Management by Walking Around), talk to your people, ask questions, and watch how things are being handled. You might gain new insights and find new opportunities that they bring to you as you pass by. You can't lead well if people never see you. You should be setting the tone for your office by being there so people can take their cues from you.

The third duty in Gookin's list may strike you as a bit odd. How, after all, can we be both a good boss and a good friend? Gookin suggests that, while it's difficult, parents can be good friends. They do it, she says, by spending time with their children. They play, laugh, and cry together. More importantly, parents accept their children for who they are. They don't harp on or point out all their weaknesses, but help them build up what they are good at. They encourage and praise, but, most importantly, they don't wait to find time for their kids—they *make the time.*

We think the same is true for managers.

Doug

When I think of the many managers I've had that were good and bad—and believe me, I've had both—I think it's easy for me to describe the differences between the two. The good managers were fun to work for. That didn't mean they were pushovers who let me get my way. In fact, it was often the opposite. But they knew when to make us work hard and when, just as importantly, to let us play hard. In short, they were there whenever I needed them, and they took a genuine interest in my needs as an individual.

The bad managers could never tell the difference. They let us play when we should be serious, and they got really serious when we needed a break. Anytime they tried to "care" about us, their efforts seemed either insincere or ill timed. And if I really needed them, that always seemed to be the time they were too busy.

The key to being a good role model, an ever-present teacher, and a good friend is consistency. Consistency isn't about being perfect, i.e., being right all the time. Instead, it's about staying true to a way of thinking and a set of principles. Just as children tolerate their parents' imperfections, so too will employees tolerate mistakes from bosses; but they tend to quickly punish inconsistency.

As a final note, we must be careful not to confuse consistency with stubbornness. There are always two sides to any story, and a manager who is a role model, teacher, and friend cannot be afraid to change an opinion or policy if given rational reasons for doing so by employees any more than a parent can risk being so obstinate with their children. Too many people think that once they make a decision, they must stand by it or they will look weak.

Doris

My father was a very strong, stubborn, and opinionated man, but he was willing to admit when he was wrong. My sister was equally strong and stubborn. Once, when she was a senior in high school, she was invited to visit her boyfriend at his college for a special college weekend. My father told her that she couldn't go since there might be too many temptations in that setting.

My sister felt that he was being very old-fashioned, as many of her friends were able to visit their boyfriends at their colleges. She went to the school guidance counselor and several teachers who understood the teenage social scene better than our father did. She got letters from several of them advising our father that he should let her go since she was a responsible and mature high-school senior. My sister gave him these letters from credible people and also reminded him that she would be going to college herself the next year and would be out of his control then. If he couldn't trust her now, how could he do so then?

He was impressed by her diligence and effort, and he had to agree with her logic. He changed his mind and allowed her to go.

Doris's sister handled the situation correctly. Instead of going head to head in a loud argument, which was how she and her father tended to interact, she got her facts together and went to him with a rational, calm request to reconsider. This put him in a cooperative rather than defensive mood and both parties ended up satisfied.

An employee should not have to be afraid to point out an error that a superior has made, but it should be done with respect. And a manager, when approached with this type of respectful, rational information, should not be afraid to reverse a decision.

Follow the platinum rule of human relations. Following the old "golden rule" of treating others as you would like to be treated yourself is old-fashioned. Today, you must treat others as they want to be treated (which might be different from the way in which you would like to be treated). Find out what motivates them to do their best and find ways to provide those incentives. Leaders don't worry about being loved or admired. They are more concerned about their followers feeling good about themselves and encourage their people to concentrate on doing the right things.

Above all, we must remember that we are normal human beings and will not ever be perfect. We will strive to be excellent, but not perfect. It can be very difficult to admit error to our subordinates, but it will greatly aid in communication and mutual trust when we are able to do so. Covering up will never work in the long run. When we have erred, blamed the wrong person, or acted in an inappropriate manner, we need to be willing to apologize. To quote Donna Jablonski, mother of an eight-year-old, in *Child Magazine,* November 1996, "You have to forgive yourself a little bit each day. No parent is perfect; all you can do is your best."

The pursuit of perfection often impedes improvement.   —George Will

Tips from Managers

1. Accept the fact that you will make mistakes.

2. Be willing to admit your mistakes.

3. Be willing to apologize when you are wrong.

4. Don't worry about things you can't control. Learn to live with them and put your energies into controlling those things that you can control.

5. Accept the fact that your employees will make honest, innocent mistakes. They are not trying to cheat you.

6. Put in systems that will help catch mistakes where possible.

7. Be open with your employees and encourage them to trust you and feel secure coming to you when they have made a mistake. They can't be perfect either.

8. Look at failure as an opportunity to learn and see what is needed to use the learned information for future success.

9. Don't waste time looking for someone to blame when something goes wrong. Work with your team to solve the problem. Then teach everyone what has been learned so the same thing won't happen again.

10. Be an honest, forward-looking, and optimistic leader.

Tips from Employees

1. Be truthful and open with us.

2. When you say you will do something, please follow through.

3. Accept that we are human as well and that we will make honest mistakes even though we are working hard.

4. Help us to avoid being afraid of admitting our mistakes.

5. Help us to learn from our mistakes.

6. When you have been unfair to us, be willing to apologize to us. We will respect you more for that.

7. When we fail, don't consider us to be failures—realize that it is just a failure of that event.

8. Help us to learn from our failures.

9. When something goes wrong, don't ask us who is responsible. We don't want to tattle on our co-workers. If you have given us an open atmosphere and we are to blame, we will come to you and admit our error if we are responsible.

10. When something goes wrong, help us solve it before spending time on finding out who did it.

CHAPTER 12

"Do as I Say, Not as I Do" Doesn't Work: Effective Role Modeling

The acorn doesn't fall too far from the tree.

Doris

When Doug and Donald were growing up, they played soccer like most kids in Bowie, Maryland. One year, we were all at a game watching Donald play. Most children's soccer organizations throughout the country group two years of kids together. Don was in his second year of playing in this age group, so he was among the oldest on the team. We were pleasantly surprised to see that his best friend at the time was playing goalkeeper for the opposing team. Close to halftime, however, I suddenly realized something must be wrong. This friend of Donald's was a year older than he, so how could he possibly be allowed in this league?

I asked the league commissioner about the situation, and she confronted the boy's mother. The mother admitted that, when she was in line for registration, she heard a parent just ahead of her being told that the twelve- to thirteen-year-old league was closed out, so she lied and told the registration people her son was eleven. This story didn't surprise us, as Phil and I knew that Donald's friend's parents were not very disciplined with their children and had a very self-centered view of the world.

The boy was asked to leave the league, and it actually cost Donald his friendship. Years later, the boys ended up in high school together. Donald was a top student while his former friend, who was equally intelligent, was constantly in trouble.

Did Donald's friend struggle as a teenager just because his parents lied about his age when he was twelve to get him into a soccer league? Of course not. But is it possible for a child to grow up believing in the value of honesty when his parents are telling him to lie because that's the only way to get what you want? Donald, though he lost a friend, learned an important lesson about the sacrifices that can result from honesty, but that it's worth it in the end. His friend didn't learn much at all.

The Importance of Role Modeling

Parenting for Dummies lists being a positive role model as one of the three duties of a parent. Sandra Hardin Gookin points out that, since children look to their parents as an example of how to behave, the parents must be positive role models. Parents must remember that their children are always watching them and will imitate their behavior—whether that behavior is positive or negative. The idea that a parent can have a "do as I say, not as I do" attitude is false and won't work in real life. Parents must be careful not to do or say anything they would not like to see or hear their child repeating in school.

Linda and Richard Eyre, authors of *3 Steps to a Strong Family,* state, "It goes without saying that the most effective way you can teach family laws is to live them yourself." This doesn't mean that all laws apply the same way to everybody. For example, courtesy and mutual respect are laws that apply to everyone in a family, but in different ways. Children not only need to let their parents know where they are going and why, but they also need to ask for permission to go. Parents obviously do not need to ask their children for permission to go someplace, but it is simple reciprocal courtesy to let their children know where they'll be.

The same is true in the office family. Courtesy and mutual respect among members of an office family are necessary elements for long-term success. Yet often, the respect is not mutual. Managers expect co-workers to work out problems in a calm, civilized manner and many demand restraint from their subordinates; yet they do not return the favor. They respond to problems with quick anger, and they deal with their employees in condescending, sarcastic, or manipulative ways. Even simple courtesies such as "please" and "thank you" get lost in their world. The Eyres point out, "It is truly shocking how we sometimes speak to our children— worse than we would speak to anyone else—as though they were . . . objects or extreme irritations." Oh, how true that can be with our office families as well!

*"You're setting a bad example for the
employees, Mrs. Lawrence."*

So what is good role modeling? Role models are people you look up to and try to be like. A good role model doesn't have to be someone who is perfect in every way. In our experience consulting with hundreds of office managers, most of whom also had children, we have found that one of the most common mistakes managers and parents make is not knowing how to be wrong or how to handle mistakes—both their own and those of their subordinates or children.

Why? For one thing, it isn't easy to tolerate mistakes. The only thing more difficult than tolerating other people's mistakes is tolerating one's own—especially when we know others are looking to us for the answers.

One of the toughest challenges in a family or office is teaching people that it's OK to make mistakes (as long as they learn from them), while at the same time not (1) making it seem as if everyone now has carte blanche to make mistakes without regard for how to avoid them and/or (2) reducing the parent's authority. In fact many parents, both at home and in the office, live under the illusion that they need to hold their "children" to standards of perfection and need to appear perfect themselves to maintain unquestioned authority.

We don't expect babies to be perfect, to come out of the womb talking, walking, and knowing right from wrong. We keep teaching them how to do new things and encouraging them along the way. The instinct is so natural to parents that even mother birds do it.

Donald

In the first home I owned, my wife and I were witness to one of the more amazing things in wildlife. A mockingbird had nested in one of the small trees in our front yard. The mother used to buzz me on my way to work since I was in "her" turf. The hassle was worth it all when, one day, we witnessed her teaching her young to fly.

It was truly fascinating to watch. The mother would demonstrate how to fly and then screech encouragement to her little offspring. When the baby bird didn't move, the mother would come back and demonstrate a shorter flight. Then she'd fly up to the roof—as if to show the rewards possible from flight—and demonstrate a series of smaller flying hops. All the while, she chirped her encouragement. When the little bird finally made a small flight, the mother seemed to congratulate the baby and then demonstrate the next, more difficult maneuver.

If we don't expect babies and children to be perfect, why then do we expect subordinates to be perfect just because they're adult? If anything, they're more challenging.

Donald

The mother and her baby struck me immediately as an object lesson in a problem I was having at work. I had a new employee who was replacing a very good marketing manager who had left recently. The new marketing manager was having problems getting up to speed. Her troubles were causing her to question her capabilities, which, in turn, was causing her to make more mistakes.

I, myself, was frustrated because I was used to handing assignments to my former employee without worrying about how they would be done. He got things done with very little help from me. It made my life a lot easier, and now I no longer had that luxury. Like many managers I've seen, I could have reacted by showing my frustration and being upset that the new person couldn't handle the full load. But the mother bird didn't expect her young to fly immediately; she had to teach the offspring one step at a time. I realized that I needed to develop the new employee, my "office baby" (even though she was older than me), one step at a time. It's the old "crawl before you walk, walk before you run" approach.

By reducing her workload in the short term, I was able to get her to take the pressure off herself and let her naturally grow into the full job. It was more effort up front for me, but the payoff was that, six months later, she was fully functioning and as competent as her predecessor. She had to go through the same growth stages I'm watching my children go through at home before she could be a fully functioning "office adult."

Many managers and parents who understand that incremental teaching is part of being a role model still fall victim to the mistaken belief that, if their "children" see them make any mistakes, it will ruin their ability to lead. Fearing that being wrong yourself will somehow undermine your authority is simply absurd. Sure, being wrong continually will undermine your credibility; but if you're a manager who's wrong that often, you probably should look for a new career anyway lest your boss beat you to that conclusion. No one, least of all your children or your subordinates, expects you to be right all the time. They know you're human.

Being wrong and unable to admit it, however, will definitely undermine credibility. Doug remembers one of his most frustrating bosses early in his career.

Doug

I had this one boss, Mary. Mary seemed to feel as if she had to be better, smarter, and more experienced than everyone else in order to be boss. I never heard her apologize to anyone or admit she was wrong. She was wrong plenty of times—she'd just never admit it out loud. Perhaps she thought admitting she could be wrong would show some sign of weakness that would be used against her. In practice, however, it reduced her effectiveness, as she became a subject of ridicule at the water cooler and often burned through people because they were tired of working for someone who was so overbearing.

Contrast this with one of his favorite bosses in his career.

Doug

Jim was the exact opposite. He practically reveled in being wrong. He was much smarter and more experienced than he ever said (I suspect he knew that). The few times he turned out to be wrong about something, he was the first to admit it. It was as if he was saying, "If it's OK for me to be wrong, then it's OK for you to be wrong. Just don't make a mistake because you waited too long, and learn from your mistakes so you don't make the same one twice." The result was that his entire team, including me, felt motivated to prove him right whenever we could.

It's difficult to acknowledge to our children—and our subordinates—that we were mistaken. "But how much it does for communication and for trust!" the Eyres say in their *3 Steps* book. "When you've made a mistake or blamed the wrong person, or gotten angry when you shouldn't have, apologize!"

Sometimes parents, in the office or the home, don't realize they're wrong until they've made complete fools of themselves. We've all seen one or more of our bosses do it—and probably our parents at some point as well. They get upset at a small transgression or they accuse, try, and convict a co-worker (or worse, you) before getting all the facts. Maybe you've even done this yourself. Though not proud of it, we have to admit that each of us has done this at least once.

The important thing to do when this happens is to apologize, or explain why you got upset. It's healthy for kids to know that their parents get upset or mad. Everyone does. How you handle being upset is what's more important. This works the same in the office as it does at home. The action itself is not what is critical; it's how you react.

Being a good role model is not always easy. Honesty can be painful. The mother who lied to let her son have a chance to play soccer wasn't necessarily a bad person. In fact, she wanted her kid to be happy and not disappointed that he couldn't play that year. But what's the collateral damage? There is often a long-term impact when standards are abandoned in favor of short-term expediency.

Successful role modeling occurs when leaders believe in "do as I do, not just as I say." This may be easy when tasks are as simple as teaching a child to walk or an employee to use the voicemail system. But it gets much more complicated when the behaviors desired are complex—such as teaching teenagers how to exercise good judgment or an employee how to sell. Doug remembers a particularly powerful lesson on how the real learning is in the role modeling, not classroom lecturing.

Doug

I had been running a particular sales organization for about three years using a traditional "ask early, ask often" approach to closing sales. As the market was getting more complex and our product more long-term-relationship oriented, it became obvious to me that we needed to move to a more sophisticated, consultative approach. The approach required a considerable amount of interactive dialogue before even bringing up contracts, prices, or other terms of sale. The challenge was how to change the behavior of salespeople who were used to selling in the traditional style.

We, of course, used classroom-style training, videos, etc., but I knew that strong role modeling was the only way we could have a chance to succeed. I spent a full two months in the field with my salespeople making joint calls. One early call really made a mark on one of the salespeople that probably still lasts to today.

We were making a joint call on a prospect who had started in our pipeline under the old method. We had qualified the prospect the old way, and were pretty sure we had a "slam dunk" if I just was willing to close the business the old way. I knew the salesperson knew this as well, and that was part of the problem. If I used the old way, I'd be sending a message that the new way isn't really how we want to do business—it's just words to be abandoned whenever it becomes expedient to do so.

Much to my employee's surprise, I took the risk of literally starting the conversation from scratch, using the new consultative approach. It took a little longer, but there were three benefits: (1) the employee saw how serious I was about our need to change, (2) the employee saw it worked, and (3) instead of gossiping with his colleagues (we all gossip about these sorts of things) about how I was saying one thing but doing another, he was going to gossip about how I stuck to my guns on the new approach.

Just as important, had I used the old method, we would have had a sale. With the new method, we had a customer. That was the whole point of the new approach, and my employee learned this with power that my words in the classroom could never convey.

For all the value that the quality of role modeling we've discussed so far brings to the table, it is equally important that parents, in both the home and office, spend a quantity of time with their children. As Kathryn Hill noted in *Child Magazine* in November 1996, "When it comes to your children, be frugal with your pennies, not with your time."

Donald had a boss who epitomized this approach.

Donald

In a consulting company I worked for, I had a team leader named Chris. Chris was one of those guys who is always calm and thoughtful. Often, I worry about people who are so quiet either being wound up too tightly inside or not being aggressive enough to tackle the tough problems, but every so often you run into one of those quiet people you just know can make things happen. They just don't wear it on their sleeve. Chris was one of those.

One of the things that made Chris such an effective team leader was that he invested time in his people. He was responsible for his own projects as well as leading the team of project managers and consultants, but he always had time for people. Every time I needed his help or just needed to vent about something, he was there. No matter how busy he was with his own projects, he never rushed me. The time invested with me and other team members translated to better performance across many projects.

Parenting books and magazines frequently decry the fact that many children are not getting the time they need from their parents. Office workers are frequently equally neglected. There's always a good excuse not to be home for the kids or in the office for employees. In the 1980s, Tom Peters (author of *In Search of Excellence* and other seminal management books) emphasized the importance of a management practice we've espoused for years—MBWA (Management by Walking Around). As he put it, when you walk around, you see what's happening, communicate interactively with your staff, and find opportunities for those special moments with your employees that are just as important as those you remember having with your parents growing up. Peters is also quick to point out that, even if you don't create those special moments, at least you're not in your office writing memos and otherwise interfering with your staff!

We've had many moments in our careers where walking around has offered that opportunity for a special moment of bonding. Donald actually had one in the middle of working on this chapter.

Donald

I was new to managing a particular project. As I was walking around just after normal hours, I came by the desk of one of my engineers to see if he was still around. He was, so I asked him how things were going. I meant it as an innocent question, but I've learned long ago to be prepared for any answer to such a question. Before I knew it, we were involved in a very serious discussion about how he was frustrated with the way his last review had gone and how small a raise he got.

He perceived that he had been misunderstood and mistreated. Here I was just making a routine, "Hi, how's it going?" visit, and suddenly this is a deep conversation. I realized that this situation was an opportunity in every positive and negative sense of the word. Handle it well, and I have a very motivated employee; dismiss it as a minor concern, and I could be contributing to his deciding to leave the company.

I listened to his complaints and we crafted a plan through which he could demonstrate performance on my project, enabling him to get the promotion I believed he deserved. I promised I'd be there for him in his next review as long as he was there for me on this project. I had only briefly worked with the person, and now we had a bond of trust that moti-vated him to go out of his way to succeed on this project. The time I spent with him reminded me of some of the special moments I had with Mom or Dad growing up. They were never planned. They just happened—but they lasted forever.

Role modeling can build positive attitudes and behaviors, but it can also transfer negative ones. This is particularly true when dealing with fear of the unknown. Instead of looking at challenges as exciting oppor-tunities, scared managers infect their staff with these fears. For example, employees may know their manager is afraid of the competition from the Internet, and they get paralyzed by that fear. They are no different from sons and daughters who sense that their mothers are afraid of lightning and then take that fear as their own.

Phil and Doris, when consulting with travel-agency owners during one of the most difficult times in the industry's history, put this observation to use.

Doris and Phil

In the mid- to late 1990s, the travel-agency industry was turned upside down as airlines slashed traditional commissions and the Internet was becoming a major factor of competition, especially for airline sales. Agencies had to learn new ways to make money—sometimes completely reorienting their business from commercial to leisure sales. Agencies were closing their doors or merging at a record pace.

Many of the agency owners who came to us for help were naturally afraid of the changes and were unsure what to do. We found three tactics that worked very well. First, as consultants, we were in the position of the "wise old grandparents." Our clients may have been office parents them-selves, but they were scared.

We put the new order in the perspective of the many years of change and reminded them of all the successes they had in the past. We talked to them about how they could apply lessons from their past to succeed in the future despite their fears. We commented to ourselves several times how it felt just like the times we had to deal with our kids being afraid of their first day in high school, going off to college, etc.

The second tactic that worked was asking them what they were saying and doing with their employees. Most admitted they were at least acting scared, and many "fessed up" to directly expressing their fears in words. Most of these clients were women business owners, and we found that the analogy of transferring fear of thunder to young daughters worked well. We encouraged them to keep talking only of the positive challenges and potential for success, no matter what their inner fears. This would help their employees and, in turn, help focus them on the positives.

The other tactic was to directly attack the assertion all these managers made that things just weren't as good as they were many years ago. We reminded them that, while computers make our lives faster paced, they also make it possible to do more business. We asked them if they remembered when all tickets had to be handwritten and agents were lucky if they could do a quarter-million dollars of business a year. We contrasted their ability to be in business today—with agents routinely selling triple what they'd been doing—if productivity was still that low. We suggested they help their employees keep a realistic perspective as well.

Those who followed our advice reported it worked so well they couldn't believe it. The depression in the office brought on by fear and pining away for earlier times just disappeared, and people went about the work at hand. In fact, many were seeing record profitability once they got refocused.

Doris and Phil's experience is repeated whenever managers verbalize how they wish for the "good old days" when the job was more "fun." However, we are firm believers that the "good old days" were not quite as "good" as they were "old." Sure, there are greater stresses throughout our society as we struggle to do more work with fewer people, and the pace of change is faster than ever. At the same time, the standard of living is higher than ever, people live longer than ever, and the same changes that add stress also provide unprecedented choice. Much as Doris and Phil saw in the story above, people also tend to have selective memories. They often gloss over any challenges of the past while focusing on just the negatives of today. As Doris and Phil pointed out, it's easy to pine for the "simplicity" of the past while forgetting what a pain it was to handwrite tickets.

When we think of the possibilities and pitfalls of role modeling, we always think of an old joke (that could be true in many homes) that really drives home how institutionally ingrained some behaviors can become.

Doris

A daughter is turning twelve, and her mother decides to teach her the ancient family recipe for cooking pot roast. She proudly shows her child how to take a pot roast, cut an inch off each end, season it with the special family-secret mixture of herbs and spices, and then cook it in the oven for four hours at 325 degrees.

"Why do we cut an inch off each end?" asks the inquisitive, yet naïve, daughter.

"I really don't know," answers her mother, who hasn't thought much about it. "That's the way my mother taught me. Let's call her to find out why."

The same dialogue is repeated as the mother calls her mother. As luck would have it, her mother's mother (the daughter's great-grandmother) is alive and well, having just celebrated her ninety-eighth birthday. When the trio asks this grande dame of the family why they cut an inch off each end of the pot roast, the great-grandmother responds with a bit of a surprised chuckle, "Because, in our first house, the oven was so small that we couldn't fit a whole pot roast in it!"

How many strange recipes for pot roast are running around your office?

Role modeling is such a powerful parenting tool that it works its wonders whether intended or not. If children are perceptive about how their parents' behavior is different from their words, imagine how perceptive adults in an office are about the disconnects between their bosses' words and actions. You can't expect people (whether they're twelve, twenty-two, or fifty-two) to embrace behaviors bosses ask them to follow while ignoring the fact that the same bosses regularly behave in ways the employees are asked not to.

These "do as I say, not as I do" behaviors simply don't work as an effective parenting strategy—at home or in the office. Just as positive, confident, caring behaviors from the office parent beget positive, confident, caring behaviors among the office children, so does hypocrisy from the office parent beget hypocrisy from the office children. The advice that Gookin gives in *Parenting for Dummies* is equally true for office managers:

1. *No cursing.* If your behavior is at odds with your words, it is your behavior that will be most imitated.

2. *No sarcasm.* If you use sarcasm to get points across to your subordinates, don't be surprised if they do the same with you and each other.

3. *No yelling.* If the boss yells, so will the staff. Yelling only increases tension and negative feelings within an office.

4. *No arguing.* It takes two people to create an argument. You can control the discussion by staying calm and maintaining a rational conversation instead of an argument that creates a win/lose environment.

This shouldn't be a surprise to anyone, yet how many managers do you know who don't seem to get it?! We've consulted with business owners who complain about how their staff members "goof off" too much and don't pay attention to the real work at hand, only to personally witness these owners constantly making personal phone calls in the office or talking about the golf round they played just the day before when the staff was in the office busily working. Maybe their ownership gives them the power to do things their staff cannot, but what kind of message does it send? Maybe they worked all weekend and needed the afternoon off to relax playing golf. But their staff doesn't know that and likely will assume the worst. It's easy enough to avoid the problem by making the personal calls at home, or at least closing the office door, and by avoiding talking about the round of golf.

Parents have to set the example if they want it followed. You wouldn't be surprised if children whose parents told them to be honest and then bragged about lying on their tax return grew up to cheat on taxes. There should be no shock, then, when employees whose managers expect honesty from them and then boast about putting something over on a customer or supplier later lie to customers or cheat on time sheets or expense reports. There should also be no surprise when a manager who considers a customer to be an interruption in their otherwise delightful day finds that their employees resent the "intrusion" of these customers. They're just following the example they saw!

The Keys to Getting Success from Subordinates

MegaSkills, written by Dorothy Rich, is a book on how families can help children succeed in school and beyond. It could just as easily be about what managers can do to help subordinates succeed. This shouldn't surprise us since the "beyond" part of "school and beyond" is the workplace. Ms. Rich lists ten critical megaskills, each of which an office or home parent can positively model.

1. *Confidence:* feeling able to do it. Demonstrate self-assurance without arrogance and encourage others to be confident in their actions.

2. *Motivation:* wanting to do it. Show that you are willing to do what it takes to get the job done. Understand what motivates your subordinates—for some it's money, others status, still others quality of life.

3. *Effort:* being willing to work hard. You can't expect others to put in the extra effort if you don't do it yourself. If your employees see you leaving the office every day at five o'clock sharp, they'll follow suit. If they hear you talk down about your customers, they'll do the same.

4. *Responsibility:* doing what's right. It's not easy to leave your kid out of soccer for a year, but the pain of honesty today pays off in integrity later in life.

5. *Initiative:* moving into action. When the going gets tough, do you get going? Or do you freeze, search for scapegoats, or have some other dysfunctional reaction? Your subordinates take their cues from you.

6. *Perseverance:* completing what you started. Thomas Edison once said that "innovation is 1 percent inspiration and 99 percent perspiration." Get your employees to stick to things even in the rough times by doing the same yourself.

7. *Caring:* showing concern for others. If you don't care about your employees, why should they care about you?

8. *Teamwork:* working with others. You want your staff to work well with each other and with you, so you need to model the behavior and do what it takes to work well with your peers and your boss.

9. *Common sense:* using good judgment. Explain your reasons for making decisions the way you do. So many parents hide information from their children, whether at home or in the office, as if secrecy makes decisions unassailable. But children and employees can't learn good decision making if they are never exposed to the process.

10. *Problem solving:* putting what you know and what you can do into action. The best way to teach people how to solve problems is to let them see how you solve yours.

In summary, bosses drive corporate culture just as parents drive family values. The single biggest contributor to the establishment and change or maintenance of these cultures and the behaviors they create is role modeling. In any situation, the parental authority is seen as a role model by all who are subordinate. Whether that parent's behaviors are good or bad, constructive or destructive, they will drive similar behaviors in the children.

Former basketball star Charles Barkley once made a commercial in which his message was that he is not a role model. Many managers feel the same way. They feel as if they are there to "get a job done"—whatever it takes. They're both wrong. You're a role model whether you like it or not. The only question is, what type of role model are you going to be?

> Children have never been good at listening to their elders, but they have never failed to imitate them.   —James Baldwin

Tips from Managers

1. Remember—your employees watch everything you do, and they pass judgment!

2. Don't do or say anything you wouldn't want your employees doing or saying.

3. Using simple courtesies like "please" and "thank you" with subordinates goes a long way towards establishing mutual respect.

4. When teaching employees new skills, don't expect them to excel immediately any more than you expect a baby to speak complete sentences.

5. Teach your employees through role modeling that it's better to admit a mistake quickly and learn from it than to let it fester. When you've made an error, confess to it and apologize if warranted.

6. Honesty really is the best policy. This may sound trite, but it's true.

7. GOYA! Get off you're a—, and walk around to see what your employees are doing. Show them you care.

8. If you are afraid of change in your industry, that's OK. But either talk about it rationally with your staff or hide your fears so you don't transfer them to your team.

9. Every morning, pick one of the ten "megaskills" and think of something you can do today to practice it.

10. Ask yourself, "Does my boss have any bad habits that I in turn am passing on to my subordinates?" If the answer is yes, change your behavior!

Tips from Employees

1. Don't be afraid to admit you made a mistake. We don't expect you to be perfect any more than we expect to be perfect ourselves.

2. If you want us to respect you, then you must respect us.

3. We want positive role models, so be one for us.

4. If you want us to learn from you, you have to be patient with our mistakes.

5. If you ask us how things are going, be prepared for an honest answer.

6. The only way we can learn from you is if you invest the time with us to teach us what you know.

7. Help us challenge the status quo to improve on how things are done. Who knows how many "pot-roast procedures" we may help you fix?

8. Most industries experience frequent change. Help us work through our fears about these uncertainties—don't add to them.

9. Closed executive doors are a surefire way to show you really aren't interested in what's going on, so don't be surprised if we don't care about what's going on with you either.

10. Show us that you genuinely care about our needs, and we'll go to the wall for yours.

CHAPTER 13

The Classic Motivation Mistake: Why Can't You Be Like Your Sister (Brother)?

If you have a baby, will you like it better than us?
>—Caption to a cartoon of a table of men
>in front of a lone businesswoman, accompanying
>an article on sibling rivalry by Ellen Goodman

Phil

Jim hired me to help him evaluate his financial management. His business wasn't doing as well as he thought it should, and he was seeking advice from me on where he could improve performance. He was smart and knowledgeable, but it seemed to him that his business was underperforming—in short, it seemed as if the whole was less than the sum of its parts.

As part of the review, I had analyzed each member of his sales and service staff. One thing I uncovered was related to his two most senior employees, Sarah and Jane. Sarah clearly worked faster but consistently made more errors, while Jane worked more slowly but more accurately. In the end, their net productivity, after the cost of Sarah's mistakes, was quite similar.

I shared this with Jim and was in his office when he met with each employee. As he was discussing her strengths and weaknesses with Sarah, Jim made the classic mistake of saying, in his most fatherly manner, "I know you pride yourself on how fast you are, but why can't you be more like Jane and get your work done with fewer mistakes? Then you'd really be adding even more value." I cringed, and I could see that Sarah, though not responding verbally, was seething.

Before he met with Jane, I shared my concerns with Jim. I told him that I understood he was trying to be helpful, but I asked him to see it from Sarah's point of view. Jim tended towards speed at the expense of details himself—why else would he make such a hasty comment to Sarah? With this quick role play, he immediately saw how upset he would be if someone told him the same thing. Besides, I told him, rather than comparing them and saying why can't you be faster like Sarah or more accurate like Jane, the key to better performance was just to help Sarah become a little more careful (although he could never get her to be as careful as Jane) and to get Jane to work a little faster (again, she'd never match Sarah's speed).

I got Jim to realize that they each had their own strengths and weaknesses. Sarah's speed led to some of the mistakes, and Jane's plodding nature avoided many. The answer was not to turn either one into the other. Rather, he needed to help each one improve on her weakness and praise her strength, without mentioning the other "sibling."

Jim proceeded to have a great meeting with Jane. He followed up by apologizing to Sarah for his inappropriate comments and just encouraged her to work as best she could on paying attention to details while not losing the speed that she was so proud of. When I followed up six months later, Sarah and Jane still had the same strengths and weaknesses but Sarah had cut her mistakes by more than half, and Jane had improved her productivity by almost 10 percent!

"Why can't you be more like your sister (brother)?" We've all heard it before. It may have been directed to us or one of our siblings, or we may have overheard it when directed to a friend by their parents. And doesn't it make our skin crawl? We may have even caught ourselves saying it. Certainly, we've all caught ourselves thinking it!

But as we discussed in an earlier chapter, no child—office or home—is supposed to be like their siblings or co-workers. They each bring their own strengths and weaknesses to the home or office, which is why parenting and management experts alike universally reject this tactic. It doesn't really motivate the person to whom it is directed to act any differently. But it can leave them resenting the parental authority for making the comparison, as well as the sibling for being "so perfect." It can even make the siblings to whom they are being compared feel uncomfortable. They may feel it gives them unwanted attention that pits them against their colleagues.

The authors of *How to Survive Your Adolescent's Adolescence* admonish us, "Parents should avoid comparative statements that pit sibling against sibling, setting up an unwanted, artificial rivalry that is often destructive to

"When I asked you to be more like Susan,
this isn't what I had in mind."

family unity. . . . Comparisons . . . are bound to create jealousy and resentment and often lead to a 'good child/bad child' attitude that may backfire as the labeling process leads [kids] to give up trying since everyone is convinced they are no good."

While misguided, the attempt to shame someone into better performance is based on our desire to motivate them. The best way to avoid this mistake is to learn more about the right way to inspire people—parenting style!

Every parent has heard these complaints: "My friend Jimmy's mother lets him do that!" "It wasn't my fault!" "Why should I have to do that?" (the unstated completion being "I won't get anything for it anyway"). These are simply the manifestations of three basic principles that children learn very early in their lives. They want "fairness," or at least their version of it. If a friend is allowed to do something, then they want to be allowed the same privileges. If a sibling gets it, they want it. As all parents know, their children's version of fairness can often omit many important facts.

Children's actions are based on who they think should be credited and/or blamed. They are motivated to seek credit and avoid blame. They may even miss opportunities to learn from mistakes if they are unwilling to recognize their own, or if parents focus too much on assessing blame rather than pointing out lessons from an experience. Adult employees can act very similarly.

Children are most motivated by what they expect to get from their actions. We like to joke that they are tuned in to their favorite radio station,

WII-FM—"What's in It for Me?" Children's natural state is one of self-centered play. Sharing is often taught in the form of "When you share your things, others will share their things with you." Work is something children are often coerced—"You're required to help out with family chores"—or "bribed" into doing—"You earn an allowance based on doing chores" (some parents even dispense with allowance and simply employ a "pay per chore" strategy). While every parent struggles against this natural tendency towards selfishness, they can use to their own advantage their children's desires to accumulate things. It doesn't even have to be money or possession oriented. Even at young ages, some children are motivated by recognition as much as or more than things. Donald's older daughter is an excellent example.

Donald

My daughter will probably grow up and kill me for putting this in the book, but it's such an interesting lesson. When my wife, Yvonne, was potty training Erika, she tried all of the things the books recommended. She showed her what to do, tried to catch the time she normally went, even let her wet herself. Nothing seemed to be working. Erika understood what was going on, but just wasn't doing anything about it.

Then Yvonne came up with the idea that some simple positive recognition was worth a shot. She put a card up on the refrigerator and bought a pack of four different colors of stars. Yvonne told Erika that every time she went potty in the toilet, Erika could pick which color star she wanted and put it on the card. The card didn't have lines or anything to track performance in the adult sense. Erika just got the privilege of picking the color and putting it wherever she wanted on the card. Within two weeks, she was completely trained!

But this wasn't the only time or way the tactic worked.

Donald

We were having some problems with Erika forgetting her "pleases" and "thank-yous" when she was five. Yvonne brought out the trusty "earn a star tactic," and everything turned around that day. Erika had matured since the last time, so she brought an interesting twist to the game this time. In a demonstration of the "fairness" she expected, she would only play the game if Mommy and Daddy also had to "earn" stars for saying "please" and "thank you."

The stakes may be a little different in the office, but the games are still the same. Management theorists have recognized the same behaviors in the office and given them official-sounding names. Equity, attribution, and expectancy theories describe adult behaviors at work in the same way parenting experts have described the situations we just discussed. This should be no surprise. Motivation is a universally human issue. The fundamentals are no more different between work and home than the people are. We're all people, and we are ultimately motivated by the same things. Some may be more sensitive to one than another, but the basics are still the same.

Equity Theory

All of us, particularly in American society, seek some form and level of social justice. That is to say that we all have some sense of what is right and wrong, fair and unfair. The determination is made by comparing a given circumstance to similar ones either experienced or learned. Newspapers and news shows like *60 Minutes* have made their living by presenting situations that seem so clearly unfair that they motivate us to feel particular emotions and maybe even to take some form of action.

Siblings, whether in the home or the office, engage in a constant search for equity—sometimes by trying to raise themselves up, other times by bringing others down. Parenting books present the scenario of a teenage sibling complaining, "Nikki got to go out three nights last week, and I only got to go out once," but how often have you seen a similar dynamic play out in your office? Never forget that the adult world isn't necessarily any more adultlike.

Parenting experts advise that the best defense is to be prepared. "But Nikki did all her homework and also cleaned out the garage. You haven't finished your term paper and haven't managed to clean up your room." This approach explains, in reasonable and unemotional terms, the rationale behind your decision. Nikki's privileges aren't better because you "like her better." She simply lived up to her responsibilities, thus providing a good lesson for all children if they wish to grasp the workings of the adult world.

The same advice works in the office. We don't recommend that managers regularly get trapped into a "scorecarding" game; however, they must understand that their subordinates frequently compare their own situations to their office siblings'. And like the home situation above, they may be very selective in the facts they use to support their judgment of what's "fair." It's only natural. Managers can't get upset. They should use their "parenting the office skills" to take some time to communicate and manage.

Attribution Theory

Our final analysis about any situation, and thus our satisfaction with the status quo or motivation to behave differently, depends on to what we "attribute" the success or failure of our performance. As early as 1968, behavioral psychologist R. DeCharmes proposed that when people consider themselves to be the "locus of causality" (a technical term for being the source of success or failure), they will be intrinsically motivated. When they consider themselves to be merely pawns in the process, they will be extrinsically motivated. This is the difference between being motivated by the rewards of the task (the joy of success, learning, etc.) versus the rewards of the outcomes (bonuses, rewards, etc.).

Simply put, when those whom we manage feel responsible for their own success, they're more likely to be successful. We've learned in our experience to add another element to this equation. Parents, both in the home and in the office, must be willing to give authority to their "children" commensurate with their responsibility. Responsibility without authority is, perhaps, briefly motivating, as the subordinate feels a new level of importance. But lack of commensurate authority soon leaves them disenchanted because they get frustrated at being held accountable for results that they lack the authority to do anything about.

This concept of driving authority down the chain of command is a critical part of the continuing trend to "flatten the pyramid" in organizations. The idea is to move from a boss (i.e., parent), directive-driven world into one where workers share a vision of what success is and are given tools and decision-making authority to achieve that success. One of its earliest proponents was Jan Carlzon, CEO of Scandinavian Airline System (SAS), who used this approach to dramatically improve customer service. As he described it in the late 1980s, "Last year, each of our 10 million customers came in contact with approximately five SAS employees, and this contact lasted an average of 15 seconds each time. Thus, SAS is 'created' in the minds of our customers 50 million times a year, 15 seconds at a time." Carlzon felt that these "moments of truth" would be responsible for the public's image of SAS. The company would succeed or fail based on this picture. These small 15-second contacts, he believed, were the opportunities that the company had to prove to the customer that they were making the right decision in choosing SAS.

Carlzon realized that SAS employees wouldn't be motivated to provide this kind of service because their boss, their office "parent," said so. They'd have no sense of ownership in the result. Only by showing them, through statements like that above, exactly how important they are in the success of the company was he able to motivate them to perform to the absolute best. When they realized that success was *attributable* to them and them alone, and they were allowed to make decisions to help customers, motivation came naturally.

Parenting expert Dorothy Rich considers motivation to be so important that she devotes a whole chapter to it as one of the ten "megaskills" needed for children to grow. While motivation can be difficult to define, she says when they have it, it shows.

1. You see your children wanting to do things.

2. They do schoolwork and household jobs without a lot of nagging.

3. They make plans for the next day or week.

4. They say yes more than they say no.

The strength of this behavior comes not from any extrinsic reward, but from the intrinsic reward of feeling in control, believing you have freedom of choice, and feeling committed. This can occur when parents guide rather than decree and managers coach rather than boss. There's no shortcut to turn an apathetic worker into an excited one, any more than there's a quick trick to turn an uncaring teen into one bubbling with enthusiasm. But the same tactics that Rich suggests parents can use to teach their progeny to be more motivated work equally well for managers and their subordinates. These lessons can help people gain the discipline required to stay motivated, to work against discouragement, and to face competition and challenge.

Managers can coach their office children on how to control their situations, so that these employees may truly be able to attribute their own success to themselves. These lessons include showing staff how to break their own jobs down into manageable bites, how to set and keep to their own time limits—and also how to give themselves a pat on the back for a job well done!

Expectancy Theory

Simply put, expectancy theory refers to motivations driven by expected outcomes. Expectancy on the job comes in many forms—salary, bonus, responsibility, promotion, vacation time, etc. Earlier in this book, Doris and Phil discussed a decision in their business to change from salary to a pure sales-commission, pay-for-performance system. It was similar to a decision they made many years earlier with Doug, Donald, and their sister, Dana, to change from a straight weekly allowance to a pay-per-chore system. In both cases, there was no obviously right or wrong answer in the absolute sense. Rather, in both situations, they realized their children—both in the office and at home—had come to expect pay independent of any performance. The result was insufficient performance due to a lack of motivation. The change reenergized both the office and the home, and the entire motivation picture improved.

We can also use expectancy theory to motivate subordinates by setting higher expectations. When we sense uncertainty, or we know we're asking an employee who tends to be afraid of new and unknown things to step out of their comfort zone, we can pump them up by simply telling them, "I know you can do this." Ken Blanchard relies on this as a critical element of his "One-Minute Reprimand." He instructs all managers to include an affirmation that "I know you know the right thing to do" whenever they deliver a reprimand for poor judgment. He understands the importance of validating people's self-assurance by reminding them that they can rely on their sense of expectation and equity to make good decisions.

Dorothy Rich reports on the power of expectations in her book *MegaSkills*. She recalls a California study that showed "ordinary" students could excel when expectations for them were high. According to Rich, researchers tested students at a school for their academic potential. The teachers were not given the results. The students then were randomly divided into two groups. The teachers were informed that one group was made up of students who had excellent potential that had not yet shown itself, but that was expected to show up within the coming year. They were what is known as "late bloomers." The students lived up to the teachers' expectations even though these expectations were based on false information.

These teachers unknowingly set higher expectations than they otherwise would have. How many managers are missing improved work from their employees because they don't set expectations that motivate them to achieve this way?

But We Can't Help But Make Comparisons!

While it's true that both home and office parents commit a major error when they compare one child to another as a tactic to change behavior, this does not mean that successful parents and managers never make comparisons. Children and employees are all different, and it is natural to make comparisons. More importantly, it's OK to realize that some children are easier to raise than others. Drs. Don Dinkmeyer and Gary McKay, in *Raising a Responsible Child,* point out, "Parents who attempt to fool themselves with the notion that they feel, or even should feel, equally accepting of all their children often become anxious when they try to accomplish this extremely difficult, if not impossible task. It's hard to feel loving toward someone who keeps 'kicking you in the shin.'"

They contend, and we agree, that parents need to admit the differences they feel and not get caught up in the turmoil of second-guessing what they "should feel." What they need to do is develop consistent approaches to dealing with all their children.

The simple fact is that all employees, and all children, are not equal. Parents are the "orchestra conductors," making sure that everything in the office or home functions as smoothly and effectively as possible. Viewing equality in its purest sense, the conductor would rotate a musician so that he played on every instrument. The result would obviously be a disaster. A conductor doesn't expect the tuba player to play the violin, just as the tuba player probably doesn't want to play the violin.

At the same time, the conductor doesn't criticize one musician for not being the same as the other. We know it takes the full orchestra to play a symphony. All the musicians get the opportunity and benefits that are the natural and logical consequences of their own innate talents coupled with the decisions they made as they pursued a musical education and career.

Doris and Phil

In our family, Donald handled money much better at a younger age than either of his siblings. We complimented him on his abilities, and we gave him more financially related responsibility and authority. While we enjoyed knowing we could rely on his unusual-for-that-age responsibility with money, we never criticized his brother and sister for not sharing that expertise, since we didn't expect these skills in them. We could have asked, "Why can't you be more like Donald?" But that would miss the point. They weren't Donald, and their skills were well within what we could normally expect.

The same situation played out in our office. Our manager, assistant manager, and we could write clear and effective letters while most of our other employees could not. Today's education does not produce adults who can all write well. Therefore, we set up a policy that major letters had to be checked by one of the four before they could be sent out. We didn't make the staff feel bad by asking them why they couldn't be more like the managers. We simply put systems in place that protected us from problems while using the skills the employees did have.

The important point is that, while everyone is not equal per se, they are "equal under the law." They are all subject to the same rules, and the responsibility/authority they receive is commensurate with the natural and logical consequences of their skills and performance. The tuba player can't fault the conductor for a violinist getting more playing time if that's what the piece calls for, any more than Donald's siblings could be upset at any benefit he gained from his advanced financial management abilities.

Similarly, our staff should not have resented the additional responsibility and authority our managers had as a result of their writing skills. We are not saying they didn't complain; but when they did, we were able to explain exactly why the situation was the way it was. If they wanted different results, then the tuba player would have to learn the violin, and our staff would have to learn to write better. Again, it's not about comparing them to each other directly; it's about the natural and logical consequences of their capability and performance.

There are other examples of how much employees can differ in abilities or styles. Some people work well only with very neat desks, while others do better with cluttered (but organized) desks.

Donald

As with most of my family, I am not a member of the "clean desk" club. In fact, the once or twice a year I clean my desk, I often amuse people by calling out, "Eureka! I struck wood!"

My first boss in the air force was much more fastidious than I. He appreciated my abilities, but I could sense he was concerned that the clutter on my desk was a sign of disorganization. I'll never forget a day that I was in the middle of working on several documents related to a large "request for proposal" for which I was responsible. I had several stacks of paper on my desk, with several more on the floor around me.

My boss came in to ask me a simple question, and he noticed what could only look like a total mess to him. He left after I answered his question but quickly returned and asked me for a particular document. I knew he didn't need the document. He obviously expected me to struggle finding it, which would be the perfect segue for him to give me a lesson on staying "organized."

What he didn't realize was that there was a method to my madness, and I did have everything under control. I immediately reached under my desk to the pile by my left foot and produced the document. To his credit, he realized that I was in control and just operated differently than he did. He never "tested" me again, and I never again felt that he was concerned about the lack of empty space on my desk.

This isn't meant to imply that messy is good. When Donald worked in a position where customers saw his desk regularly, he kept it much cleaner because he didn't want them to misinterpret his abilities. The point is that individuals have their own styles and office parents should focus on the substance, not the style, of their subordinates.

But Wait, There's More

Motivation theory alone does not sufficiently describe the forces behind our children's/subordinates' behaviors. They, like all people, have differing personalities. Some are leaders, and some are followers. The former are referred to in psychological terms as allocentric, the latter as psychocentric. Allocentric people are trendsetters. They are the first to try something new, whether they are the child trying a new sport or an employee trying to master a new task. Psychocentrics do not want to try anything new until they are sure of what it is like. The psychocentric waits for friends to do something and will follow whatever is in fashion. Simply put, psychocentrics are at ease only when within their comfort zone, while allocentrics are driven to leave their comfort zone on a regular basis.

Most people, of course, are midcentric, falling somewhere in the middle of this scale. Judging where your children or employees fall on this scale will help you better understand their personalities and prepare them for what lies ahead.

Education is also a key part of motivation. Whether a child at home or an adult at work, humans are motivated by learning and the opportunity for growth that comes with it. Parenting and management books alike are filled with advice to teach children and employees one thing or another. One of Carlzon's most famous quotes is "An individual without information cannot take responsibility; an individual who is given information cannot help but take responsibility."

Training is equally important in the office as it is with our nation's youth. Learning doesn't stop at home, and continued education is the cornerstone of the modern organization's efforts to support personnel. Without general education, employees cannot possibly be equipped to handle the fast pace of change in business and society. Without specific training on the processes involved with a particular company and its products, even the most talented people will fall flat on their faces.

Doris and Phil

Talking to other parents and business owners/managers, we continue to hear the same refrain over and over. Everyone wants to know what the "secret" is to good parenting or good management. It seems as if everyone thinks there is a magic potion or a silver bullet—that one thing they need to learn to be effective or the three things that, if they taught their subordinates, would make everything easy.

We're here to tell you there is no such thing. "Magic pixie dust" may work for Peter Pan, but it doesn't exist in the real world. The "secret," if there is one, is that you don't have to be 100 to 200 percent better than everyone else at 1 or 2 things to be a superparent or supermanager. You do have to be 1 or 2 percent better on 100 to 200 things. Constant attention to detail and performance of the "little things" are what is critical to success. Maybe that's where the challenge is. It's simple to focus on just 1 or 2 things. It's very challenging to pay attention to 100-plus things!

A Final Word on Comparisons

We've talked about why office parents shouldn't fall prey to the "Why can't you be more like . . ." to compare employees directly to their office-mates. There's a similar classic mistake to avoid. As parents, many of us desperately want our children to be like us. This pattern also occurs in the office, but it is important not to compare a subordinate's way of doing things to the way you would do them, as long as they work.

Phil

In the early 1980s, I was a manager at a trade association. I promoted a person, who had been a trainer in the field, to a supervisory position. She hired a new trainer to replace herself on the road. Unfortunately, she expected the new trainer to use her style in training and continually compared the way the new trainer worked to the way she would have preferred, even though the new person's methods were perfectly appropriate, just different.

The evaluations the new trainer received from her students were equally as high as her supervisor had received. After a few weeks, the new trainer asked me if she was doing a good job, and, if so, could I "get her boss off her back." After some one-on-one counseling, her supervisor did ease up. But their working relationship was never what it could have been, and the new trainer left the association about a year later.

This failure to recognize that very different styles can still achieve the same results is a problem many new managers face.

Doug

I had been a salesperson for several years before I had the opportunity to manage other salespeople. One of the most frustrating experiences I had initially was realizing how much better I could have handled a situation than the junior salespeople I had working for me.

Fortunately, I had a mentor who gave me some of the best advice I've ever received as a manager. She reminded me that, as a manager, my success wasn't going to come from my direct sales skills. It was going to come from my ability to train and motivate others to sell. She reminded me that, when I was less experienced, I learned some lessons the hard way myself.

These talks gave me the perspective I needed to avoid unfairly comparing them to me and enabled me to look for the unique traits that would allow each to succeed.

That is probably the single most important lesson to be learned from this entire chapter. Just as parents must let children grow according to their own skills and capabilities, so, too, must office managers give their employees the opportunity to succeed in their own way.

Contrary to what you may think, your company will be a lot more productive if you refuse to tolerate competition among your employees.
—Alfie Kohn
management lecturer and author

Tips from Managers

1. Realize that each employee is different, and let them express their differences in their work.

2. Avoid making comparative statements verbally.

3. Understand that all employees seek "fairness."

4. Don't get caught up in "scorecarding," but do be consistent in the application of your judgment and support.

5. Give employees a sense of ownership, responsibility, and authority—it's very motivating.

6. Build up your employees' expectations. Expectations, high or low, are often self-fulfilling.

7. It's OK to "feel" differently about different subordinates—just treat them equivalently.

8. Equivalent treatment is *not* equal treatment, but employees should receive the natural and logical consequences of their performance.

9. Understand that some employees are comfortable leaving their comfort zone and some are only comfortable in their comfort zone. Assign tasks with this in mind.

10. Judge subordinates' job performance on what they do and the results of their actions, not on how closely it compared to the way you would have done it.

Tips from Employees

1. Treat each of us as individuals with our own strengths and weaknesses.

2. Let us play to our own strengths rather than trying to mold us specifically in your own image.

3. We know you can't help but compare us to our peers, but don't tell us about it. Counsel us as individuals, not by telling us to be more like somebody who is a peer.

4. At the same time, if there is somebody ahead of us in the organization who demonstrates the abilities we should aspire to, by all means tell us how we stack up against them. There's a big difference between comparing us to another "parent" in a different part of the company and comparing us to our office siblings.

5. Share as much information as you can with us to help us avoid drawing the wrong conclusions. We know we don't know all the facts about ourselves and our officemates, but it's hard to avoid making fairness judgments based on what we do know.

6. When we handle responsibility and authority well, give us more.

7. Share with us what you expect from us. Don't give us much more than we can handle, but don't be afraid to push us. We'll let you know if we can't handle it.

8. It's OK to "feel" differently towards your employees—just be willing and prepared to work with any of us.

9. Treat us "equally under the law," not equal in the strictest sense.

10. We know we have a tendency to stay in our comfort zone. Push us a little bit out of it anytime you can. (Actually, most of us hate admitting this, because we'd really rather stay in our comfort zone; but, in the end, we'll thank you for it.)

CHAPTER 14

The Single Parent: What to Do
When the Buck Stops with You

Strange, when you ask anyone's advice, you see yourself what is right.
—Selma O. Lagerlof
Jerusalem

Phil

One of our earliest clients, Joanne, had opened up her own travel agency about two years before she came to us. She had been a wonderful agent herself in another agency and had decided that she could do a better job for her clients if she could run her own agency. However, she really hadn't understood what running a business was all about. She had thought that, as long as she sold a lot of travel and kept her clients happy, her business would automatically succeed financially.

She had hired one other person to help her. Together, they met with the clients and sold travel. At home in the evenings, Joanne would enter all sales, receipts, and payments for that day into a spreadsheet. This worked fairly well while there were just the two of them in the office and business was at a level they could handle together.

However, since Joanne and her employee were both good salespeople, the business started to grow. They needed to bring on a second employee and Joanne now had to spend time training this new, inexperienced person. With three people handling clients, Joanne was less familiar with every transaction, and she was still responsible for her previous clients. She was coming home at night much more tired, yet still had to enter the financial data herself. In addition, her simple spreadsheet entries informed her of the day's sales volume and commissions, money deposited in the bank, and the total sum of the checks paid out, but she was not capturing what she needed to really understand what was happening in her business. She was beginning to feel out of control.

This was the point at which she called on us for help. This, in itself, was a very smart move—not so much that she called on us, but that she realized that she needed outside help—that she couldn't do everything herself. She was beginning to be owned by the business, rather than the other way around. She was finding herself frustrated, tired, and losing patience with her employees when they needed her help. She simply had too much on her plate.

The first thing we did was to introduce her to an accounting system that was specifically designed for travel agencies and taught her how to use it. This took care of her being out of touch with what was happening in her business, but it didn't yet ease her work burden. We also referred her to an accountant in her area who understood travel-industry accounting, and she outsourced her end-of-year accounting and taxes to this expert. He was also able to advise her during the year on special accounting and financial questions.

The next thing we did was help her realize that she had to start delegating some of her work to one of her employees. She had to teach them how to do some new tasks and then trust them to do the job as she had taught them. She could not continue to serve a full client list and manage the company effectively at the same time.

With an outside expert assisting with financial needs, and her subordinates sharing the rest of the load, Joanne was now able to devote some time to managerial tasks, such as assisting her staff, where needed, and planning for the future.

If you are a "single parent" or the sole manager of a business or office, your job can be especially difficult. You have no one else to turn to—no one who can take the burden off your shoulders, even for a short time. You're it! You have to do everything, be Mommy and Daddy and still find time to meet your personal needs. How does a single parent do it all? The answers to this question are directly applicable to the only thing almost as difficult as being a single parent—being a single manager. You are a "single office parent" if you are the owner or manager of a small business or manager of an office that is autonomous, where you must be chief executive officer, chief operating officer, chief financial officer, and sometimes even chief janitorial officer!

In the ideal situation, parenting is something that should be shared. Just as raising children is a time-consuming, difficult, and sometimes frustrating task, so too is managing employees. It is very hard for one person to do it alone. However, just as our society has experienced a growth of single-parent families, we also have seen a great growth in small businesses, many of which have just a single owner/manager.

Even in big business, pressures to "flatten the pyramid" and "downsize" (or the more politically correct "rightsize") have left traditional managers feeling more as though they're alone on a ledge. This type of single-manager situation, where the manager runs a department in a larger business, is more like the single-parent family living close to relatives. These office parents face many of the challenges and frustrations of single parents, but at a less intense level. A parent living in close proximity to other relatives at least has grandparents, uncles, or aunts who can help out in emergencies and on those "really bad days." Managers who run an office within a large company similarly have peers and bosses they can easily turn to for advice or assistance or just to vent.

Challenges Facing the Single Parent

Sole managers of small businesses have to be jacks of all trades. They face decisions requiring a variety of talents and knowledge. They are the heads of the personnel, marketing, finance, strategic planning, and all other departments.

It is impossible for one person to have the necessary expertise, let alone the time, to be effective in all areas. Therefore, it is critical that such managers find the help they need from others. They need to be effective at delegating. They must teach their employees how to help out with chores necessary to run the business. They may even outsource some tasks to consultants or other companies, thus freeing their time to spend on the tasks for which they are most qualified.

In the story that opened this chapter, we had to teach Joanne to become a manager. A good manager, like a good parent, teaches their employees how to do tasks necessary to maintain the business so that, as they grow, they will be able to do more and more themselves. It is not the parents' job to do everything, but rather to help their children to grow and to develop new capabilities and skills. A manager must also know when the skills are not present in the family and outside help is needed to accomplish necessary tasks.

We could have suggested that Joanne hire a bookkeeper rather than contract with the outside accountant, but this would have given her a major additional expense—considerably more than she would spend on the outside accountant. The automated accounting system and the accountant saved her time and provided her with the information about her business that she needed for planning.

If you are a single manager, determine your greatest strengths, and put your time into those. Hire others, either on staff or as outside consultants, to help with those tasks of which you are not as capable. Look for talents within your staff and delegate jobs to employees who are best suited to achieve success in those areas.

The single manager of a department within a larger company does not usually have this set of challenges to the same degree. Most departmental managers have a focused set of responsibilities, with other departments taking care of functions such as accounting, information management, janitorial, marketing, etc. However, to run the department effectively, such managers must still understand those functions and be able to inter-act with these other departments.

Loneliness

Being a single parent can be a lonely existence. You can be friends with

"You can always spot the single managers at these seminars."

your staff, but if you get too close, you will risk other problems. It is easy to lean on one of your employees and treat that person almost as a surrogate co-manager, but this is extremely unhealthy for the well-being of the overall office. No matter how much you like your staff, it is sometimes lonely at the top. You have to make decisions that may not please everyone or that may involve confidential information that you cannot share. Good parents sometimes make tough decisions about their children, and it's no different in the office.

It's also lonely on those "bad days" when you just wish you could close the door and keep the rest of the world out so you could concentrate on your own activities, or even just rest for a little while.

Doris

When our children were younger and still living at home, there were many times that either Phil or I were very happy that we were co-parents. Luckily, rarely did we both feel down or have that bad day at the same time. We learned that whichever one of us just wasn't feeling up to dealing with the needs or demands of the kids could pass it off onto the other. We discussed many times how fortunate we were to have this outlet.

The children also learned at an early age that there were times when it was better to go to me or, at other times, to Phil. They could look at us and know right away that this was not the time to come to one of us and, wisely, go to the more "up" parent that day. They also knew that for certain types of help, they were better off coming to the one who was their best resource.

If I was tired, I could ask Phil to watch the kids while I rested, and he could do the same with me. When we have a co-parent on site, we frequently take this support and shared responsibility for granted.

We often found that the same dynamic played out at the office. We were able to share the load, with Phil more responsible for marketing and strategic planning and me more responsible for tactical implementation and employee morale. Even though I was usually the person employees would come to for help, they (our office "children") could tell there were days when they were better off going to Phil. And there were days either one of us could rely on the other.

It is critical that single managers find their own support systems for these situations. Although they won't have the luxury to go lie down and rest (or just stay home for the day) when they're feeling tired and frustrated, they can find others to whom they can go when an employee comes to them for help that is outside their expertise. They must develop a network of people to whom they can turn for help, so when an employee comes to them, they, in turn, can go to the right person in their network before giving the employee an answer. Sometimes just being able to talk things out with someone else who understands your situation can go a long way towards solving the problem.

In fact, in our consulting business, we have a number of clients who use us for just this type of support. They know they can call us for advice on almost anything, and we will either be able to give them the answer or send them to the right place for it. Sometimes, they just need to know they're doing the right thing or are on the right track. Moral support is very important when you're just not sure that what you're doing is right.

Single managers have to be more focused and must set up procedures for how decisions will be handled in their absence, since there is not another co-manager left in the office. However, the lack of a co-manager should not be used as an excuse for not being able to leave the office. Just as parents must leave the children on their own (once they are old enough) when both are out, employees must be trained and then trusted to handle the office in the absence of the manager.

Then, managers must make time to get out to meetings and seminars, where they can talk with other managers in similar situations. Here they can network and develop their own peer support groups. They can learn how others handle various situations and they can share experiences with others in similar positions.

We've often recommended to our single-manager clients that they join local chapters of their trade association, chamber of commerce, etc. Even if formal education programs are not exactly what they're looking for, the informal sharing of questions and concerns at these meetings can be very helpful. When they are confronted with a challenge they feel unable to handle, they've heard how someone else has handled a similar situation and/or have someone to call for advice and support.

Single parents must also find time for periodic vacations to recharge their energy. Managers who pride themselves on never taking a vacation so that they never have to leave the office are not very effective managers, even when they think they are. People need a periodic change of pace and a chance to relax.

Doris
We have a friend who had managed her business for more than six years without ever taking a vacation. She was thinking of joining one of our groups for a

cruise. It was a simple weekend getaway, all of three days away from the business. She agonized over the decision and then determined she couldn't "take the risk." We pointed out to her the importance of balance in life. "What's the point of owning your own business, if you're always chained to it?" we asked. We also reminded her that no one, not even she, was so important that the earth would end in the three days she was to miss. At the last minute, she actually decided to go. She and her husband had the time of their lives. For the first time in years, they had a chance to relax and just enjoy life. They returned refreshed and renewed.

The moral of the story is not that she had a great time but that she learned that it was OK to leave everyone in her business on their own for a few days. They survived, and so did the business. At the time we are writing this book, she's already put a deposit down on her third annual vacation in a row!

It is so easy to get bogged down in handling crisis after crisis that you can lose sight of the goals. By getting away, you can think, plan, and refocus your energies on what is important. If you never get away to be with other managers or even just to take that vacation, you will begin to resent your employees and their demands on your time and energy.

Parents who don't get away from the children periodically to have their own fun, but who are always serving the children's needs, eventually resent the children. As recommended in *Smartparenting,* by Dr. Peter Favaro, "Be sure to program some decompression time into every week. You must allow yourself to do things that are enjoyable, even selfish." Favaro pointed out that people who devoted their lives to work and children, at the expense of their own interests, would eventually come to resent both. This in turn, he noted, would increase the stress and make them less effective parents (managers).

When you find that an employee's need for you feels like an interference in your day, you have waited too long to get away. Meetings and seminars are excellent ways to get away and yet also gain information that will help you run the business better. As Stephen R. Covey states in *Seven Habits of Highly Effectively People,* we must take the time to "sharpen the saw."

Who Keeps You Motivated?

One of the responsibilities managers have is to praise and encourage their employees, but in most offices, there is no one there to praise and encourage the manager. That is one of the reasons for finding other managers with whom to meet. They can commend your good work and give you confidence in what you're doing.

All managers should read business-oriented books and articles to continually increase their knowledge and abilities, but single managers especially need to do so. They can learn a lot from reading about other people's experiences and challenges. Again, this helps compensate for that feeling of being alone.

Jack of All Trades

It is impossible to be an expert on all facets of running a business. However, you can be expert in one or two areas and learn to understand the basics in the other areas. When you outsource help in an area where you are not as knowledgeable, or you hire an employee to handle that segment for you, you will at least understand what they are doing, even if you couldn't do all of it as well yourself. You don't want to become captive to an employee or a consultant, or you could be in danger.

For example, parents who aren't expert carpenters need to hire one to build a complex set of built-in shelves. However, they can hammer in a nail to hang a picture on the wall. Similarly, you may not be able to handle all the accounting functions in the business, but you should be able to read and understand the financial statements that your accountant prepares for you and to ask intelligent questions if something seems out of order.

Organization Is Critical

For the single manager or parent, organizational skills are critical. It is amazing how much time you save throughout the day if you take a moment to plan first. "You Control Your Life by Controlling Your Time" is the title to chapter 1 of Hyrum W. Smith's book, *The Ten Natural Laws of Successful Time and Life Management.* A couple of interesting side notes—Hyrum Smith is the creator of the Franklin Day Planner®, and the subtitle to this excellent book is *Proven Strategies for Increased Productivity and Inner Peace.* If there's one thing needed by single parents, office and home alike, it's inner peace!

Keep a written list of what you have to do in both the short and long term. Remember, there may be short-term tasks that you can do now that will help you get to the long-term goals you have listed. Covey's discussion in *Seven Habits* of the difference between the urgency and the importance of tasks is another excellent resource for single parents. Prioritize your lists, so you can concentrate on the most urgent and important functions. After you have completed items based on both their urgency and their importance, you can go on to those of secondary importance. Also, ask yourself if there is a way that any of these tasks can be delegated to a subordinate. If there is, do it.

If you do not keep a daily list, you will find yourself reacting to every desire of each employee and customer without consideration of the importance of the request in the overall scheme. You will take on far more tasks that could have been delegated than if you had put in some planning time. A single parent must be even more careful of the use of each minute in the day than a co-manager since there are so many more managerial functions that must be handled by that one person. An exhausted, frustrated leader never helped any business succeed in the long run. It is up to you to make sure that you manage yourself and your time so that you are able to help your employees manage their time as well.

There may come a point when it is impossible for you, as a single manager, to complete all the tasks that you have assigned yourself. At that time, it may be best to either hire someone or promote a qualified current employee to the position of assistant manager to help you with these. You will be amazed at the relief you will feel with a co-parent sharing the load.

> The good points [of single parenting] are that you don't have to argue with a partner over parenting issues—you just do what you want. . . . The bad point of single parenting is that you don't have anyone to help you.
>
> —Sandra Hardin Gookin
> *Parenting for Dummies*

Tips from Managers

1. Understand your own strengths and weaknesses. Use your strengths and hire others to fill in your weaknesses.

2. Seek opportunities to meet with other people in similar positions to form your own support group.

3. Attend seminars and conferences to learn from others how to handle your challenges—both personal and business.

4. Read books and articles that will help you understand more about the areas of business that are not already your expertise.

5. Do not treat your employees as surrogate co-parents.

6. Make some personal time for yourself to recharge your batteries.

7. Prioritize your tasks daily and work on the most important ones. Let the lesser ones slide until the higher priorities are completed.

8. Step back periodically to regain perspective on the larger picture.

9. Delegate tasks that can be performed by employees to free your time for managerial needs.

10. Hire or promote someone as co-manager when the need arises.

Tips from Employees

1. We can help, but please don't pile every task that you don't want to do onto us.

2. Let us know when you are overwhelmed. We want to help you and, if we are caught up with our critical assignments, we'll be happy to take some things off your plate.

3. Don't be afraid to delegate meaningful functions to us that you don't have the time to do.

4. Try to be patient with us when we have a bad day and we will reciprocate on your bad days.

5. If you are not going to be in the office, please make sure you have given someone full information on anything that might come up that we will have to handle. Also, please give us a phone number where we can reach you if possible.

6. Let us know your schedule so we won't get concerned if you are late or absent.

7. Don't burden us with worries about the business just because you have no one else to share them with.

8. Remember that, although we want to be friendly, we are your employees, not your close, personal friends. We don't want to know too much about your personal life.

9. Concentrate your time and efforts on managerial matters and let us handle the day-to-day frontline activities. We need your leadership. If you are too busy doing work we can do, you won't have the energy to lead us.

10. Don't feel that you can't ever leave the office since you are the only manager. Get out and go to meetings. Bring back new ideas. We will be fine. Trust us to run the office in your absence.

Epilogue

Beware of people who tell you they manufacture antiques.

—Jim Rohn
noted self-help guru

What in the world does that quote have to do with our topic, parenting the office, you ask? In the course of our lives and careers, the four of us have read many self-help and management books. So many of them seem to be saying that they've found the Holy Grail—the one principle, or set of principles, that is new and different from all the rest—the one way that will now lead you from the darkness you dwell in to the light that you seek.

But as we've said in so many of our seminars, "There's no such thing as magic pixie dust." There is no one way to get what you need. As comforting as that would be, it's as much a myth as never-never land. In chapter 13 we shared what we've found to be the secret to success. It isn't doing 1 or 2 things 100 to 200 percent better. Rather, it comes from doing 100 to 200 things 1 or 2 percent better. It's about applying some basic fundamentals across a wide range of situations.

Now that we've written a self-help and management book ourselves, we still have the same opinion. We haven't created something that wasn't already there. Family and social behavior is older than history itself. It is, therefore, no surprise to us that the same dynamics that play out in the social unit we call a family also play out in the social unit we call the office. The former are ingrained in our psyche and culture from many millennia of human existence. The latter are a creation of the last 100 to 200 years. It's no wonder the ingrained behaviors of cooperating and competing within the family worm their way into our cooperation and competition at work.

If you leave this book with nothing else, we want you to leave with the realization that the same basic things parents teach their children are equally effective for teaching employees how to succeed. Management experts may wrap them up in fancy names and sophisticated terminology designed to separate the "learned few" from the "ignorant masses," but we find it better to just keep things simple:

1. Communicate.

2. Play nice.

3. Get along with others.

These simple, some might even say trite, fundamentals formed the basis of how Doris and Phil taught Donald, Douglas, and their sister, Dana; and they are the basis of what they taught in their office as well. In a world full of so many mixed messages about who is successful and what behaviors are appropriate, we find these three to be timeless. If you and your subordinates communicate with each other, play nice (i.e., play hard but fair and think about how your actions affect theirs), and get along with each other, your entire team will be successful.

From our office families to yours, we wish you the best of success!

Remember that management is really just "adult day care."
—advice repeated by one of Donald's colleagues

Additional Quotes

As we were researching this book, we came across many quotes on parenting and management. Some didn't make it because there wasn't enough space and others because they weren't exactly in the theme of the book. But we found them informative and often inspiring nonetheless. Here, then, for your enjoyment are some of the "backroom" clippings that we've brought back from the (virtual) cutting-room floor.

First and foremost as a manager or supervisor . . . your job is to get things done through other people. . . . You are paid to manage, not perform every task.
—Mary Ann Allison, V.P. of CitiCorp
Eric Allison, financial writer
Managing Up, Managing Down

The mature woman . . . after having raised her children has been a "chief

executive officer" at home for ten years or more. No one told her whether to dust first or make the beds first—and both chores got done.
—Peter Drucker
noted author and management expert

In order for me to look good, everybody around me has to look good.
—Doris Drury
chair of Federal Reserve] Bank, Kansas City

To be effective, a manager must accept a decreasing degree of direct control.
—Eric Flamholtz, University of California at Los Angeles
Yvonne Randle, consultant
The Inner Game of Management

The myth of efficiency lies in the assumption that the most efficient manager is ipso facto the most effective; actually the most efficient manager working on the wrong task will not be effective.   —R. Alec Mackenzie
management consultant and author

If you make an honest mistake, the company will be very forgiving. Treat it as a training expense and learn from it.   —Konosuke Matsushita
founder of Matsushita Electric Company

Until we believe that the expert in any job is the person performing it, we shall forever limit the potential of that person.   —Rene McPherson
CEO of Dana Corporation

The front-line supervisor is probably the strongest motivating or de-motivating element of all.   —Harvey Miller
co-owner of Quill Corporation

Doing what you were good at . . . is not the job. . . . Helping other people improve their performance—not doing their job for them—is what management is.   —Susan Miller
director of editorial development
of Scripps Howard Newspapers

Command is lonely.   —Gen. Colin Powell
secretary of state

And beware, . . . managers: the moment you hire your first employee, you become—whether you like it or not—a surrogate parent.
—Joan Iaconetti
First-Time Manager

As the mother of three feisty pre-schoolers, I have always contended that the best training for diplomatic service is motherhood. Who is better skilled than mothers at keeping the peace, compromising between battling factions, making everyone happy—plus being cheerleaders, morale boosters and healers of hurt feelings? Let's face it: world leaders have been known to act just like 3-year-olds.
—Julia Sharma
in a letter to the editor of
Newsweek, March 3, 1997

Because of their agelong training in human relations—for that is what feminine intuition really is—women have a special contribution to make to any group enterprise.
—Margaret Mead

Nobody can make you feel inferior without your consent.
—Eleanor Roosevelt

A lot of us who came of age in the 1960s are very wary of authority. But you can't be your child's friend; you have to turn into a parent.
—Wendy Schulman

If you have made mistakes . . . there is always another chance for you. . . . You may have a fresh start any moment you choose, for this thing we call "failure" is not the falling down, but the staying down.   —Mary Pickford

If you [employees] screw up, just tell us about it; don't worry about it. We're all in this together, and we don't know what we're doing either, so come on and join in.
—Fritz Maytag
president of Anchor Brewing Company,
as quoted in *Harvard Business Review*,
July/August 1986